PRAYING GOD'S WORD

Henry McBride

authorHOUSE®

AuthorHouse™
1663 Liberty Drive
Bloomington, IN 47403
www.authorhouse.com
Phone: 1 (800) 839-8640

Published by AuthorHouse 09/04/2015

ISBN: 978-1-5049-3437-4 (sc)
ISBN: 978-1-5049-3438-1 (e)

Print information available on the last page.

This book is printed on acid-free paper.

CONTENTS

INTRODUCTION

Two thousand years ago, Christians were given a unique gift never known before. That gift was the free and unfettered access to God's presence through Jesus Christ, but after twenty-plus centuries, what has become of prayer? Too often we find the modern prayer has been reduced to "life boat" prayers for rescue from a serious (or not so serious) plight, or to a shopping list of needs and desires. In churches the pulpit prayers are reduced to a list of suggestions on how the Creator of the universe should act.

How did it come to this? Certainly it's not for lack of "how to" books on the topic. Modern book shelves are full of ready-made advice on how to pray. To read book jackets on the subject one would think a few easy steps can open up a prayer life to immediate serene bliss. But really, we know it's not that easy, don't we?

Instead we feel guilty that our 21st century lifestyle won't allow us (if we were willing) to pray for hours a day like our Christian forbearers. Stories of Martin Luther or Jonathan Edwards' hours of prayer lead us to self-reproach more than inspire us. So the question is raised: What should we pray and how should we do it? If Fredrik Wisloff is correct in saying "You can pray all day and still not pray, yet pray for a moment and be in touch with Christ all day", what do we do to attain that connection with our Lord?

Why not the Scriptures themselves? St. Augustine called them letters from home. The writer of Hebrews tells us the Word of God is living, active and discerns the thoughts and intentions of the heart. Jesus himself promised that if we pray in his name we will be heard and what better way to do that than the very words of the Bible?

In this volume, Henry has taken the Epistles with their prayers, theology and exhortations and turned them into devotional prayers. I invite you to take this treasure, incorporate it into your daily worship and be confident you are praying according to God's will.

C. Andrew Woods

ACKNOWLEDGEMENTS

I would like to thank:

My lovely wife Nell, for her encouragement and for being my sounding board

My daughter Sarah, for her inspiration and professional expertise

My son Isaac, for his courage which also motivated me

My good friend Andy Woods, for his input and development of the text

Most important, I thank my Savior, Jesus Christ for saving a "wretch like me"

Henry McBride

FOREWORD

I am not many of the things that one would expect from a writer of a spiritual book, most certainly not an example. However, I believe in the transformational power of prayer and am persuaded that if the writers of the epistles prayed for, gave council to, admonished and gave advice in their writings, how could it be wrong to use their very words in supplication to our Master?

As is obvious, I believe that every word, every "jot" and "tittle" and every precept of Scripture is true and immutable. However, there are a number of verses I have omitted from the Epistles that in my ineptitude, found too difficult to render into the form of a germane, intelligible and relevant prayer. This of course is not to say that these verses do not possess inestimable worth inasmuch as; all Scripture is God-breathed and is useful for teaching, rebuking, correcting and training in righteousness (2 Timothy 3:16). It was simply too great a task for a layman like me.

I remember a preacher once saying that "God can draw a straight line with a crooked stick." Although not necessarily biblical, it gave me the courage to make this endeavor. It is not my purpose to present any form of new translation or even a scholarly attempt to make commentary on scriptures, instead it is merely me finding a way to speak to the God of Heaven in the language He speaks to us. This volume should never be used as any form of substitute for Holy Writ, or for a mindless reading of rote prayers to assuage guilt over the scarcity of prayer. Instead, it is my desire to provide for others the same fullness I have felt in praying in accordance with God's word.

ABOUT THE AUTHOR

Henry McBride is a layman who was born, raised and primarily educated in Evansville, Indiana, where he currently resides. His 25 plus years in southern law enforcement as well as his involvement in the development of lesson plans for high liability/risk law enforcement has motivated him to speak of the infinite value of and the practical daily application of God's Word in our ongoing march to a final spiritual victory. Henry's very personal tragedies and loss in his own family, as well as his law enforcement community, has given him an urgency to help others realize that our life is but a vapor that appears for a short time and then vanishes. Consequently, how should we then speak to the God of Heaven?

The Book of Romans

1*1, 2 & 3*Thank you, Mighty God, for the gospel you promised beforehand through your prophets in the Holy Scriptures regarding your son, Jesus. *4* Glory to you, Jesus, because through the Spirit of Holiness you were declared, with power, to be the Son of God by your resurrection from the dead. *5 & 6*Jesus, I thank you, because through you and for your name's sake, I have received grace. I have also received from you the call to obedience that comes from faith. Praise you, for now I am now among those who are called to belong to you.

*7*I pray that I may continue to receive your grace and peace, Father. *9* Teach me to serve you with my whole heart, to be a witness to the gospel and remember to constantly pray. *11 & 12*Encourage me to impart some spiritual gift to other believers to make them strong so that we may be mutually encouraged by each other's faith.

*16*I pray that you cause me to never be ashamed of the gospel, because it is your power for the salvation of everyone who believes. *17*Bless you, Mighty God, for in the gospel a righteousness from you is revealed that is by faith from first to last, just as it is written: "The righteous will live by faith." *18 & 19*Keep me ever aware that your wrath is being revealed from heaven against all the godlessness and wickedness of men who suppress the truth by their wickedness; because what may be known about you has been made plain to them by you. *20*I praise you, Mighty God, for since the creation of the world your invisible qualities, your eternal power and your divine nature have been clearly seen and understood from what has been made, so that I and all others are without excuse.

2*1*I pray that you keep me ever mindful that I am without excuse if I pass judgment on someone else. For at whatever point I judge others, I am condemning myself if I pass judgment and do the same things. *2*Father, I know that your judgment against those who do such things is based on truth. *3*So when I, a mere man, pass judgment on others and yet do the same things, how can I possibly think that I will escape your judgment? [4]I also pray to never show contempt for your tolerance, your patience or the riches of your kindness. Help me to realize that your kindness O' God leads me toward repentance.

[5]Keep me aware my Father, that if I have a stubborn unrepentant heart, I am only storing up judgment against myself for the day of your wrath; when your righteous judgment will be revealed. [6]Let me not forget that you will give to each person according to what he has done. [7] Thank you for the truth that if I am persistent in doing good and seek your glory, your honor and immortality, you will give me eternal life. [8]Let me also remember that if I am one of those who is self-seeking or rejects the truth and follows evil, there will be wrath and anger.

[9-11]Teach me to always bear in mind that there will be trouble and distress for me and every human being who does evil, but glory, honor and peace will be mine along with everyone else who does good; for you, Mighty God, do not show favoritism.

3[3]Lord, help me to realize that if I do not have faith, it will not nullify your faithfulness. [4]Let me recognize that you are true and every man a liar, so that you may be proved right when you speak and prevail when you judge. [10 & 1] I pray to fully grasp the truth, that there is no one righteous, not even one; there is no one who understands and no one who seeks you Master. [12]We all have turned away, we all have together become worthless; there is no one who does good, not even one. [13]Our throats are but open graves, our tongues practice deceit and the poison of vipers is on our lips. [14-17]Illuminate for me that our mouths are full of cursing and bitterness, our feet are swift to shed blood; ruin and misery mark our ways and the way of peace we do not know. [18] I recognize, Mighty God, that there is no fear of you before our eyes. [19]Now I know that whatever the law states, it relates to those who are under the law and as a result, every mouth will be silenced and the whole world will be held accountable to you. [20]Therefore, no one will be declared righteous in your sight by observing the law; instead, it is through the law that I become conscious of sin.

*21 & 22*Merciful God, I thank you that your righteousness, apart from law, comes through faith in Jesus and has been made known to me and to all who believe. *23 & 24*Praise you Father, that even though we all have sinned and fall short of your glory, we are now justified freely by your grace through the redemption that came by our Savior Jesus Christ. *25* Bless you, Jesus, for presenting yourself as a sacrifice of atonement through faith in your blood. I am grateful that you did this to demonstrate your justice, because in your forbearance, you had left the sins committed beforehand unpunished. *26*Thank you, Father, for being long-suffering to demonstrate your justice at the present time. This proves that you are both just and the justifier of those who have faith in Jesus.

5*/*Father, I am in your debt, because I am justified through faith and therefore have peace with you through my Lord Jesus Christ. *2*Thank you, Jesus, that through you I have gained access by faith into the grace in which I now stand and I rejoice in the hope of your glory. *3 & 4*Teach me also to rejoice in my sufferings, because I know that suffering produces perseverance; perseverance produces character and character produces hope. *5*Let me remember that hope will never disappoint me, because you Mighty God, have poured out your love into my heart by the Holy Spirit, whom you have given to me.

*6*Jesus, I give you praise, because at just the right time, when I was still powerless, you died for me and all the ungodly. *7 & 8*I know, Master, that very rarely will anyone die for a righteous man, though for a good man someone might possibly dare to die; but you demonstrated your own love for me in this: While I was yet still a sinner, you died for me. *9*I am so grateful that I have now been justified by your blood and how much more shall I be saved from wrath through you, Lord! *10*For if, when I was one of God's enemies, I was reconciled through your death, then how much more shall I be saved through your life!

*12*Let me not forget that sin entered the world through one man, and death through sin; it is in this way death came to me and all men, because we all have sinned. *15*Merciful Father, I praise you because your gift is not like the trespass. For if the many died by the trespass of the one man, how much more does your grace and the gift of your one son Jesus, overflow to me and others!

6¹Jesus, may I always consider that if I died to sin, how can I live in it any longer? ³ Help me to fully grasp that when I was baptized in your name, I was baptized into your death. ⁴I pray that since I was buried in baptism into death, I too may be raised from the dead to also live a new life through your glory Father. ⁵Teach me, Jesus, to embrace the truth that if I have been united with you like this in your death; I will certainly also be united with you in your resurrection. ⁶ & ⁷Keep me conscious that if my old nature was crucified with you so that the body of sin might be done away with, I should no longer be a slave to sin because anyone who has died has been freed from sin.

⁸Heavenly Father, I believe that I died with Jesus and that I will also live with him. ⁹I know that since Jesus was raised from the dead, he cannot die again; death no longer has mastery over him. ¹⁰The death he died, he died to sin once for all; but the life he lives, he lives to you Mighty God. ¹¹In the same way, my King, teach me to count myself dead to sin, but alive to you through Christ Jesus. ¹²Therefore, I will not let sin reign in my mortal body so that I obey its evil desires. ¹³I will not offer the parts of my body to sin as instruments of wickedness, but rather I will offer myself to you, O' God. ¹⁴Remind me often, I pray, that sin shall not be my master; because I am not under the law, but under grace. ¹⁵By no means, however, shall I ever commit a sin just because I am in grace instead of under the law!

¹⁶ Father, keep me conscious that when I offer myself to someone to obey him as a slave, I am a slave to the one whom I obey; whether I am a slave to sin, which leads to death; or to obedience, which leads to righteousness. ¹⁷Thanks be to you, O' God, that though I used to be a slave to sin, I now wholeheartedly obey the form of teaching to which I was entrusted. ¹⁸Hallelujah, I have been set free from sin and have become a slave to righteousness! ¹⁹Help me, I pray to grasp that just as I used to offer the parts of my body in slavery to impurity and to

ever-increasing wickedness, so now I should offer them in slavery to righteousness, leading to holiness.

20 & 21 Lord, remind me often that when I was free from the control of righteousness and a slave to sin, that the only benefit of doing the things I am now ashamed of was death. *22*Bless you, Mighty God, because now that I have been set free from sin and have become your slave; the benefit I reap lead to holiness and the result is eternal life. *23*Lord, keep me ever vigilant that the wages of sin is death, but your gift, is eternal life in Christ Jesus.

7*1 & 4*I know, Jesus, that the law has authority over a man only as long as he lives. I also know that I died to the law through your body, so that I now belong to you since you were raised from the dead in order that I might bear fruit to God. *5* Keep me aware of the fact that when I was controlled by the sinful nature, the sinful passions aroused by the law were at work in my body, so that I bore fruit for death. *6*Thank you, Master, that now by dying to what once bound me, I have been released from the law so that I serve in the new way of the Spirit, and not in the old way of the written code.

*7*I recognize Lord that the law is certainly not sin! Indeed, I would not have known what sin was except through the law. For I would not have known what coveting really was if the law had not said, "Do not covet." *8*Illuminate for me, the reality that sin, seizing the opportunity afforded by the commandment, produced in me every kind of covetous desire. For apart from law, sin is dead. *9*At one time, I was alive apart from law; but when the commandment came, sin sprang to life and I died. *10*I found that the very commandment that was intended to bring life actually brought death. *11*For sin, seizing the opportunity afforded by the commandment, deceived me, and through the commandment put me to death. *12* Keep me mindful that the law and the commandments are holy, righteous and good.

*14*Father, I know that the law is spiritual and I am unspiritual; sold as a slave to sin. *15-17*Help me understand that the reason I do the things I hate and do not do the good things in the law, is because it is no longer I myself who does it, but it is sin living in me. *18* Keep me aware, Master, that nothing good lives in my sinful nature; for even though I have the desire to do what is good, on my own, I cannot carry it out. *22-23*In my inner being I delight in your law, but I see another law at work in the members of my body, waging war against the law of my mind. It makes me a prisoner of the law of sin at work within my members. *24-25*Thank you, Father, that through Jesus Christ my Lord, you will rescue a wretch like me from the body of death! My prayer is that you keep me aware of the distinction, that in my mind I am a slave to your law, but in the sinful nature, I am a slave to the law of sin.

REFLECTIONS

8$^{1-2}$Jesus, I am thankful that in you, there is no condemnation. Because it is through you that the law of the Spirit of life has set me free from the law of sin and death. $^{3-4}$Praise you, Mighty God, for what the law was powerless to do, in that it was weakened by the sinful nature, you did by sending your own Son in the likeness of sinful man to be a sin offering. Help me to grasp the deep truth, that in order that the righteous requirements of the law might be fully met, Jesus condemned sin in sinful man. I am truly thankful, Lord, that because of what you did, I no longer live according to the sinful nature, but according to the Spirit. ^{5}Let me not forget that if I live according to the sinful nature, my mind will be set on what that nature desires; but if I live in accordance with the Spirit, I will have my mind set on what the Spirit desires.

^{6} Thank you, Master, that even though the mind of sinful man is death; the mind controlled by the Spirit is life and peace. ^{7}Compel me, Father, to remember that my sinful mind is hostile to you and that it will not submit to your law, nor can it do so. $^{8-9}$Encourage me with the truth that even though those controlled by the sinful nature cannot please you; I however, am not controlled by the sinful nature, but by your Spirit, if I let him live in me. Keep me aware, Lord Jesus, that if I do not have your Spirit, I do not belong to you. ^{10}Help me to always recognize that if you are in me, my body is dead because of sin, yet my spirit is alive because of your righteousness. ^{11}Bless you, my King, because the same Spirit who raised Jesus from the dead is living in me and that same Spirit will also give life to my mortal body.

$^{12-14}$Jesus, remind me often of my obligation that I must not live according to my sinful nature because if I do, I will die. Help me to put to death the misdeeds of my body so I will truly live, because only those who are led by the Spirit of God are sons of God.

^{15}Thank you for not giving me a spirit that makes me a slave again to fear, but rather giving me the Spirit of sonship and by that Spirit I now cry to you- *"Abba,* Father." ^{16}Praise you, Father, for that Holy Spirit testifies with my spirit that I am a child of yours. ^{17} Increase my understanding that if I am your child, then I am your heir and a co-heir with Christ and His glory, if indeed I share in his sufferings.

[18]I pray that you train me to consider my present sufferings as unworthy of comparing to the glory that will be revealed in me. [26-27]Thank you, Holy Spirit, for helping me in my weakness, because when I do not know what I ought to pray for, you intercede for me with groans that words cannot express in accordance with God's will.

[28]I honor you, Mighty God, because I know that all things work for the good of those who love you; who have been called according to your purpose. [29] Keep me conscious that I should be conformed to the likeness of Jesus because you predestined that I should do so. [30]Help me remember that I was called and justified to one day be glorified. [31-32]Encourage me, Lord, with the truth that if you are for me, then who could be against me; because if you did not spare your own Son, but instead gave him up for me, then how could you not also, along with him, graciously give me all things?

[33]Help me understand that as one you have chosen, who could dare to bring any charge against me, since it is you who justifies me? [34]Lord Jesus, let me truly grasp that since you died for me and more than that, are raised from the dead and are at the right hand of the Father making intercession for me, who has the right to condemn me? [35]I glorify you because neither trouble, nor hardship or persecution or famine or nakedness or danger or sword can separate me from you. [36-37]Even though it is written: "For your sake we face death all day long; we are considered as sheep to be slaughtered", in all these things you make me more than a conqueror through your love. [38-39]Thank you, Jesus, that not any power; death nor life, angels or demons, the present or the future, neither height nor depth, nor anything else in all creation, will be able to separate me from your love.

9 [19-20]Remind me, Lord, to never be impudent with you and remember the saying, "Shall what is formed say to him who formed it, why did you make me like this?" [21]Let me bear in mind that the potter has the right to make out of the same lump of clay some pottery for noble purposes and some for common use. *²²*Cause me to consider, that instead of choosing to show your wrath and to make your power known to the objects that were prepared for destruction; you bore with them with great patience and you did this to make the riches of your glory known to the objects of your mercy, whom you prepared in advance for glory

10*¹*Heavenly Father, I pray for Israel that they may be saved. *⁴*Jesus, cause them to see that you are the end of the law so that there may be righteousness for everyone who believes. *⁸*Help me proclaim in faith that, "The word is near you; it is in your mouth and in your heart." *⁹*Let me boldly declare to others that, if you confess with your mouth, "Jesus is Lord," and believe in your heart that God raised him from the dead, you will be saved. *¹⁰*How wonderful it is that with our heart we believe and are justified and it is with our mouth that we confess and are saved! *¹¹*As the Scripture says, "Anyone who trusts in him will never be put to shame."

*¹²⁻¹³*Master, I am truly grateful that there is no difference between Jew and Gentile and that you are the same Lord of all, who richly blesses all who call on you because everyone who calls on your name will be saved." *¹⁴⁻¹⁵*Compel me to consider; how can people call on you, if they have not believed in you and how can people believe in you if they have not heard of you? Let me further weigh the question, how can people hear without someone preaching to them and how can they preach unless they are sent? May it burn in my heart that it is written, "How beautiful are the feet of those who bring good news!"

11*²²⁻²³*Lord, cause me, to consider your kindness to me, as well as your sternness to the nation of Israel, who were cut off from the root. Keep me aware that I must continue in your kindness otherwise, I too will be cut off. Contrariwise, I pray that Israel ceases their unbelief, so that they will be grafted back in, because you are able to graft them in again. *²⁸⁻²⁹*Father, help me to grasp the dichotomy that only as far as the gospel is concerned, are the Jews are enemies on Jesus' account.

However, as far as election is concerned, they are loved by you on account of the patriarchs, because your gifts and your calling, Mighty God, are irrevocable.

*30-31*Let me never become haughty and forget that I was at one time disobedient to you and have now received mercy as a result of Israel's disobedience. I also pray for Israel, since they too have now become disobedient and now may receive mercy as a result of your mercy to me. *32*I beseech you to keep me from overlooking the truth that you have bound all men over to disobedience so that you may have mercy on us all.

*33*Oh, the depth of your rich wisdom and knowledge, O' God! How unsearchable are your judgments, and your paths beyond tracing out! *34*Who has known your mind or who has been your counselor? *35*Who has ever given to you, that you should repay him? *36*Glory be yours forever and ever; for from you, through you and in you are all things!

12*1*Heavenly Father, in view of your mercy, urge me to offer my body as a living sacrifice, holy and pleasing to you which is my spiritual act of worship. *2* Strengthen me to not conform any longer to the pattern of this world, but be transformed by the renewing of my mind. Show me that if I do, then I will be able to test and approve what your good, pleasing and perfect will is. *3*Teach me not to think of myself more highly than I ought, but rather think of myself with sober judgment, in accordance with the measure of faith you have given me.

*4-5*Jesus, let me never forget that just as I have a body with many parts, and these parts do not all have the same function: in you, we who are many, form one body and each part belongs to all the others. *6* Illuminate for me that we have different gifts, according to the grace you have given us. Help me to see that if a man's gift is prophesying, let him use it in proportion to his faith. *7-8*If it is serving, let him serve; if it is teaching, let him teach; if it is encouraging, let him encourage; if it is contributing to the needs of others, let him give generously; if it is leadership, let him govern diligently; if it is showing mercy, let him do it cheerfully.

[9]Cause me to recognize that love must be sincere and that I must hate what is evil while clinging to what is good. [10]Compel me to be devoted to others in brotherly love and honor them above myself. [11]Lord, let me never be lacking in zeal, but keep my spiritual fervor in serving you.

[12] Teach me to be joyful in hope, patient in affliction and faithful in prayer. [13] Remind me often to share with your people who are in need and to practice hospitality. [14] Teach me to bless those who persecute me and not curse them. [15]Encourage me, I pray, to rejoice with those who rejoice and mourn with those who mourn. [16]Let me learn from my heart to live in harmony with others and to not be proud or conceited, but rather be willing to associate with people of low position.

[17]Master, may I never repay anyone evil for evil, but instead be careful to do what is right in the eyes of everybody. [18]If it is possible, as far as it depends on me, let me live at peace with everyone. [19]Convict me to never take revenge, but leave room for your wrath, for it is written: "It is mine to avenge; I will repay," says the Lord. [20]On the contrary, my King, help me to follow your instructions that if my enemy is hungry, feed him; if he is thirsty, give him something to drink. In doing this, I will heap burning coals on his head. [21]Jesus, never let me be overcome by evil, but overcome evil with good.

13[1]Encourage me, Master, to submit myself to the governing authorities, for there is no authority that exists except that which you have established. [2]Consequently, if I rebel against authority; I am rebelling against what you, Mighty God, have instituted and if I do so; I will bring judgment on myself. [3]Let me always keep in mind that rulers hold no terror for those who do right, but for those who do wrong and if I want to be free from fear of the one in authority, then I should do what is right and I will be commended. [4] Remind me that they are your servants to do good for me, but if I do wrong I should be afraid, for they do not bear the sword for nothing. Help me to keep in mind that they are an agent of your wrath to bring punishment on the wrongdoer. [5]Therefore, it is necessary for me to submit to the authorities, not only because of possible punishment but also because of conscience. [6]Teach me to see this is also why I pay taxes, for the authorities are your servants, who give their full time to governing. [7]Compel me, I pray, to always give everyone what I owe them: If I owe taxes or revenue to pay it; if I owe respect or honor, then I should give it.

[8] Encourage me daily to let no debt remain outstanding; except the continuing debt to love others, because if I love my fellow man, I will be fulfilling the law. [9]Help me to realize that the commandments are summed up in this one rule: "Love your neighbor as yourself." [10]Give me the wisdom to grasp that love does no harm to its neighbor and therefore love is the fulfillment of the law. [11] Cause me to do this, understanding the present time and bearing in mind that the hour has come for me to wake up from my slumber, because my salvation is nearer now than when I first believed. [12]Master, I see that the night is nearly over and the day is almost here, so help me to put aside any deeds of darkness and put on the armor of light. [13-14]Strengthen me, so that I will not think about how to gratify the desires of the sinful nature, but rather to always behave decently, as I would in the daytime and to clothe myself with you Lord Jesus.

14[1]Master, remind me to accept those whose faith is weak, without passing judgment on disputable matters. [2]Help me to realize that one man's faith allows him to eat everything, but another man, whose faith is weak, eats only vegetables. [3]May I always keep in mind that one must not condemn the other; for you have accepted them both. [4]Let me consider who am I to judge someone else's servant? To his own master he stands or falls and he will stand, for you Lord are able to make him stand.

[5]Father, I know that one man considers one day more sacred than another and another considers every day alike, but teach me to be fully convinced in my own mind. [6]Let me recognize that the one who regards one day as special, does so to you and the one who eats meat or abstains, does so to you and gives thanks. [7] Increase my understanding that none of us live or die to ourselves alone. [8]If I live, I live to you Lord and if I die, I die to you; so whether I live or die, I belong to you.

[9]Keep me mindful that the very reason you died and returned to life was so that you would be the Lord of both the dead and the living. [10]Teach me, I pray, not to look down on or judge my Christian brother, for we will all stand before your judgment seat. [11]Let me not forget that it is written: "As surely as I live says the Lord, every knee will bow before me; every tongue will confess to God." [12]So then, help me to realize that I will give an account of myself to you, Master. [13]Therefore, let me remember to not pass judgment on others, but instead be fully convinced in my own mind of who you are and what you require.

[14]Lord Jesus, I am fully convinced that no food is unclean in itself, but if anyone regards something as unclean, then for them it is unclean. [15]Keep me conscious that if my brother is distressed because of what I eat, I am no longer acting in love. Compel me not to destroy my brother, for whom you died, by my eating. [16]Do not allow me, in what I consider good, to be spoken of as evil. [17-18]Illuminate for me that your kingdom is not a matter of eating and drinking, but of righteousness, peace and joy in the Holy Spirit, because anyone who serves Jesus in this way is pleasing to you and approved by men.

[19]Lord, strengthen me to make every effort to do what leads to peace and to mutual edification. [20]Let me not destroy your work for the sake of food. All food is clean, but it is wrong for me to eat anything that causes someone else to stumble. [21]Remind me that it is better not to eat meat or drink wine, or to do anything else that will cause my brother to fall. [22-23]Lord, whatever I believe about these things, show me how to keep them between you and me. Keep me mindful that the man who does not condemn himself by what he approves is blessed, but the man who has doubts is condemned because it is not from faith; and everything that does not come from faith is sin.

15[1] Teach me, Jesus, to bear with the failings of the weak and not please only myself. [2] Show me how to please my neighbor for their good and how to build them up. [3]Remind me often, Lord, that you did not please yourself, but rather you allowed the insults of those who accused me to fall on you. [4] Keep me aware that everything that was written in the past was written to teach me, so that through endurance and the encouragement of the Scriptures I might have hope.

*5-6*Give me endurance and encourage me to have a spirit of unity among other believers as we follow you, Jesus, so that with one heart and mouth we may glorify God the Father. *7*Teach me to accept others just as you accepted me, in order to bring praise to God. *13* Fill me, O' God of Hope, with joy and peace as I trust in you, so that I may overflow with hope by the power of the Holy Spirit.

16*17*Holy Spirit, help me to keep a watch out for and keep away from those who cause divisions and put obstacles in my way that are contrary to the teaching I have learned. *18*Remind me that such people are not serving you, Lord Jesus, but are rather serving their own appetites and deceive the minds of naive people with smooth talk and flattery.

*19*Guide me, I pray, to be wise about what is good, and innocent about what is evil. *20* Thank you, Mighty God, that you will soon crush Satan under your feet and that the grace of Jesus will be with me. *25-26* Praise you for establishing me with the gospel and the proclamation of your Son Jesus. Bless you for making known to me the mystery hidden for long ages past. Thank you for exposing it to me through the prophetic writings that are by your command, so that I and all nations might believe and obey you. *27*To you, the only wise God, be glory forever through Jesus Christ! Amen.

REFLECTIONS

The Book of 1ˢᵗ Corinthians

1 *⁴* I thank you Heavenly Father for your grace given to me in your Son Christ Jesus. *⁵*For in Him, I have been enriched in every way. *⁷*Because of you Jesus, I do not lack any spiritual gift as I eagerly wait for you to be revealed. *⁸*I know that you will keep me strong to the end, so that I will be blameless on that day. *⁹* Praise you Mighty God because you have called me into fellowship with your Son Jesus and because you are faithful.

*¹⁰*I pray Lord Jesus to guide us of your church to agree with one another, so that there may be no divisions and that we may be perfectly united in mind as well as in thought in your name. *¹⁸*For the message of the cross is foolishness to those who are perishing, but to us who are being saved it is your power Mighty God. *¹⁹*Help me to remember that you said: "I will destroy the wisdom of the wise and the intelligence of the intelligent I will frustrate."

*²⁰*Cause me to consider Father: where is the wise man, or the scholar, or the philosopher of this age and have you not made foolish the wisdom of this world? *²¹*Help me to grasp that the world's wisdom does not know you, but in your wisdom you are pleased to save us who believe through the "foolishness" of what is being preached. *²²⁻²⁴*Keep me conscious that even though some demand miraculous signs and others look for wisdom, I should preach Christ crucified; which may be a stumbling block or foolishness to the world, but to those of us whom you have called, it is power and wisdom. *²⁵*Let me never forget that your "foolishness" is wiser than any man's wisdom, and your "weakness" is stronger than any man's strength.

*²⁶⁻²⁷*Lord, I pray that you cause me to remember what I was when I was called. I was not wise by human standards, nor influential and not of noble birth, but you chose the foolish things of the world to shame the wise and you chose the weak things of the world to shame the strong.

[28-29]Master, you chose the lowly and despised things of this world, as well as the things that are not, to nullify the things that are; so that no one may boast before you. [30]Thank you Father, for it is because of you that I am in Christ Jesus, who has become for me your wisdom which is: righteousness, holiness and my redemption. [31]Therefore, as it is written: "Let him who boasts boast in the Lord."

2[1-2]Jesus, give me the resolve to never merely sound like I am speaking with eloquence or superior wisdom when I proclaim my testimony, but rather let me speak of nothing more than you and your crucifixion. [3-5]Remind me that the message and the preaching are not to be with wise and persuasive words, but with fear and much trembling and with a demonstration of the Spirit's power, so that other's faith might not rest on men's wisdom, but on your power.

[6-7] Help me to grasp that I do however speak a message of wisdom among the mature. It is not the wisdom of this age, or of the rulers of this age who are coming to nothing, but rather your secret wisdom. It is a wisdom that has been hidden and destined for our glory before time began. [8]Lord Jesus, may I always appreciate your brilliance in that if the rulers of this age understood your wisdom, they would have never have crucified you.

[9-10]Encourage me Father, that even though it is written: "No eye has seen, no ear has heard, no mind has conceived what God has prepared for those who love him", you have revealed it to me by your Spirit and your Holy Spirit searches all things, even your deep things. [11]For who among men knows the thoughts of a man except the man's spirit within him? In the same way no one knows your thoughts except your Holy Spirit.

[12]Keep me mindful I pray that I have not received the spirit of the world, but rather I have received the Holy Spirit so that I can understand what you have freely given me. [13]Teach me to always speak of this, not in words taught to me by human wisdom, but in words taught by the Spirit, expressing spiritual truths in spiritual words. [14] Help me to realize that

a man without the Holy Spirit does not accept the things that come from you because they are foolishness to him and he cannot understand them, because they are spiritually discerned. [15]Show me Father as a spiritual man how to make judgment about all things, but not be subject to any man's judgment. [16]Let me learn in my heart that even though the Scriptures say "Who has known the mind of the Lord that he may instruct him?" you have given me the mind of Christ.

3[1]My Father, encourage my spiritual growth so that I will not remain a spiritual infant. [2]Let me crave solid food, not just spiritual milk, and cause me to be ready for it. [3]Train me not to be worldly, or act like a mere man by being jealous or quarreling with my brothers. [6]Help me to grasp that some plant the seed of faith, others may water it, but you my King, make it grow. [7]I pray that I will grasp the truth that neither he who plants, nor he who waters is anything, but it is only you, who makes things grow. [8]Encourage me with the truth that the one who plants and the one who waters have one purpose, and each will be rewarded according to his own labor. [9]For we are your fellow workers in your field and in your building.

[10-11] Show me my Lord Jesus how to be careful in building on the foundation that was laid in my heart, which is you. [12-13]Teach me to use gold, silver and costly stones on this foundation not wood, hay or straw, because my work will be shown for what it is, when the Day brings it to light. Cause me to consider that my work will be revealed with fire, and the fire will test the quality of each man's work. [14]If what I have built survives, I will receive my reward. [15]If it is burned up, I will suffer loss; I know I will be saved, but only as one escaping through the flames.

[16]I pray that you train me to realize that I am your temple and that the Holy Spirit lives in me. [17]Help me to understand that if I destroy your temple, I will be destroyed because your temple is sacred and I am that temple. [18]Father do not let me deceive myself, if I start to think that I am wise by the standards of this age, cause me to become a "fool" so that I may become wise. [19-20] Illuminate for me how the wisdom of this world is futile foolishness in your sight and how you catch the wise in their own craftiness. [21-23]Thank you Lord because in you, all things are mine,

whether it is the world, or life, or death, or the present or the future, they are all are mine because of Jesus Christ.

4¹ Thank you Jesus for allowing me to be one of your servants and entrusting me with the secret things of God. ²Keep me aware that it is required of those who have been given a trust to prove themselves faithful. ³⁻⁴Encourage me not to be concerned about other's judgments, or that of any human court, or my self judgments; because even though my conscience is clear, that does not make me innocent, it will be you who judges me. ⁵Teach me therefore to judge nothing before the appointed time, but rather wait till you return. I exalt you Father because you will bring to light what is hidden in darkness and will expose the motives of men's hearts, after which we will receive your praise.

⁶Teach me Lord to apply myself the meaning of the saying, "Do not go beyond what is written" so that I will not take pride in myself over others. ⁷Help me realize that I am no different from anyone else because; what do I have that I did not receive and if I received it, how can I boast as though I did not? ¹²⁻¹³Remind me to work hard with my own hands and when I am cursed, I should bless; if I am persecuted, I should endure it; when I am slandered, I should answer kindly even if I am treated like the refuse of the world.

5⁶Keep me mindful Jesus that not only is boasting not good for me, but a little yeast works through the whole batch of dough. ⁷Show me how to get rid of the old yeast so that I may be a new batch without yeast like you really are; because you are my Passover lamb that was sacrificed. ⁸ Help me to keep the "Festival", not with the old yeast, which is the yeast of malice and wickedness, but with bread without yeast, which is the bread of sincerity and truth.

⁹⁻¹³Father God help me realize that you will judge the people of this world that are outside of the church and for me to keep from associating with them I would have to leave this world, but I must not associate, or even eat with anyone who calls himself a brother who is sexually immoral

or greedy or an idolater or a slanderer, a drunkard or a swindler. Let me not forget the admonition "Expel the wicked man from among you."

6/I pray that if I ever have a dispute with a member of the church that you would compel me to take it before the saints and not the ungodly for judgment. *2-3*Cause me to realize that you said that the saints will not only judge the world, but also the angels, and if we are to judge the world, are we not competent to judge trivial cases and the things of this life? *4-5*May your church realize that even men of little account in the church are wise enough to judge a dispute between believers. *6-8* Illuminate for me the truth that if we have lawsuits among us in front of unbelievers we are defeated already. Instead it would be better to be cheated and wronged than for us to do the same to our brothers.

9-10 Keep me I pray to be ever mindful that the wicked will not inherit your kingdom O' God. This includes the sexually immoral, idolaters, adulterers, male prostitutes, homosexual offenders, thieves, the greedy, drunkards, slanderers and swindlers. *11*Thank you Lord Jesus, even though I was at one time some of those things, you washed me, sanctified me and justified me in your name and by the Holy Spirit of our God.

*12*May I always bear in mind that although everything is "permissible" to me, everything is not beneficial, nor should I be mastered by anything. *13*"Food for the stomach and the stomach for food", but you will destroy them both. My body is not meant for sexual immorality, it is meant for you and you are meant for my body. *14*Thank you Father that you raised Jesus from the dead and by your great power, you will raise me also. *15*Lord Jesus, keep me conscious I pray, that my body is one of your members and that I should never unite it with any kind of sexual immorality. *17*Instead I should unite myself with you so that I can be one with you in spirit. *18*Help me to flee from all sexual immorality, because all other sins I commit are outside my body, but if I sin sexually, I sin against my own body. *19-20*Compel me Lord to realize that my body is a temple of the Holy Spirit who lives in me, whom I have received from you and since I am not my own, but was bought at a price; I should always honor you with my body.

7²³Heavenly Father, let me never forget that I was bought at a price and I should never become a slave of men. *²⁴*I pray that you show me how to remain in the situation you called me to and how to be responsible to you. *²⁹⁻* *³¹*Help me to see that the time is short and that this world in its present form is passing away. *^{32 & 35}*I pray that you keep me free from worldly concern and show me daily how I can please you with my undivided devotion.

8¹Father God, let me not forget that I possess knowledge and knowledge puffs up, but love builds up. *²⁻³*I pray that you keep me conscious of the truism that: "the man who thinks he knows something does not yet know as he ought to know", but if I love you; I will be known by you. *⁴*Master, I know that an idol is nothing at all in the world and that there is only one true God, which is you.

*⁵⁻⁶*Even though for some people there are many so-called "gods" and "lords", whether in heaven or on earth, yet for me, you are the one true God, my Father, along with my Lord Jesus Christ from whom all things came and for whom I now live. *⁷*Help me to realize that some people are still so accustomed to "idols" that when they see certain practices, they think of them as pertaining to an "idol"; and since their conscience is weak, it is defiled. *⁸*Keep me aware that these practices do not bring someone nearer to you and that they are no better or worse if they observe them.

*⁹*Cause me I pray to be careful however, that the exercise of my freedom does not become a stumbling block to the weak. *¹⁰⁻¹¹*Help me to see that if anyone with a weak conscience sees me exercising this knowledge, that it is possible that they would become emboldened "to eat what has been sacrificed to idols" and consequently this weak brother, for whom Christ died, would be destroyed by my awareness. *¹²*Let me see when I sin against my brother in this way and wound their weak conscience, I sin against you Jesus. *¹³*Teach me to understand that if any of my behavior causes my brother to fall into sin, to never do it again, so that I will not cause him to fall.

REFLECTIONS

9⁷Cause me to consider that no soldier serves at his own expense, nor does anyone plant a vineyard, or tend a flock and not eat of its grapes, or drink of the milk. *⁸⁻⁹*I know that this is not merely from a human point of view because it is written in the Law of Moses: "Do not muzzle an ox while it is treading out the grain" and is it not about mere oxen that you are concerned. *¹⁰*Surely Father this was written for me, because when the plowman plows and the thresher threshes, they ought to do so in the hope of sharing in the harvest. *¹³*Let me learn by heart that those who work in the temple get their food from the temple, and those who serve at the altar share in what is offered on the altar. *¹⁴*In the same way Lord, you have commanded that those who preach the gospel should receive their living from the gospel.

*¹⁹*Father, even though I am free and belong to no man, give me the strength to make myself a slave to everyone; to win as many as possible. *²⁰⁻²¹*Teach me to become like those under the law to win those under the law, and to be like those without the law to win those without the law. In every case keep me conscious that I am not under the law, but I am under your law and that of Jesus too. *²²*I pray that to the weak I become weak, to win the weak and therefore become all things to all men so that by all possible means I might save some. *²³* Help me to realize that I should do all this for the sake of the gospel so that I may share in it's blessings. *²⁴*Show me how to appreciate the truism; that in a race all the runners run, but only one gets the prize and that I should run in such a way as to get the prize.

*²⁵*Let me not forget that everyone who competes in the games goes into strict training and they do it to get a crown that will not last; but I should do it to get a crown that will last forever. *²⁶⁻²⁷*Lord, may I therefore not run like a man running aimlessly, or fight like a man beating the air, but instead teach me to beat my body and make it my slave so that after I have preached to others, I myself will not be disqualified for the prize.

10¹Lord teach me to not be ignorant of the fact that the Israelites were all under the cloud and that they all passed through the sea. ²They were all baptized into Moses in the cloud and in the sea. *³-⁴*They all ate the same spiritual food and drank the same spiritual drink; for they drank from the spiritual rock that accompanied them and that rock was Christ Jesus. *⁵*Nevertheless Father God, you were not pleased with most of them and their bodies were scattered over the desert. *⁶* Illuminate for me that these things occurred as an example to keep me from setting my heart on evil things as they did. *⁷*Keep me from being an idolater, as some of them were; as it is written: "The people sat down to eat and drink and got up to indulge in pagan revelry." *⁸*Strengthen me I pray, to never commit sexual immorality, as some of them did and in one day twenty-three thousand of them died. *⁹*Guide me to never test you Lord, as some of them did and were killed by snakes. *¹⁰*Also compel me not to grumble, as some of them did and were killed by the destroying angel.

*¹¹*Father, let me recognize that these things happened to Israel as examples and were written down as a warning for me, on whom the fulfillment of the ages has come. *¹²*Master, encourage me when I think I am standing firm to be careful so that I don't fall! *¹³*Help me grasp that no temptation has seized me except what is common to man and that you are faithful to not let me be tempted beyond what I can bear. Thank you Lord that when I am tempted, you will always provide a way out so that I can stand up under it. *¹⁴-¹⁶*Because of this Jesus, urge me to flee from every form of idolatry and understand that the bread we break, along with the cup of blessing for which we give thanks, is a participation in your body and blood.

*¹⁸*Cause me Lord to consider the people of Israel and the fact that those who ate the sacrifices participated in the altar. *¹⁹-²⁰*I know that a sacrifice offered to an idol, or the idol itself is not anything, but the sacrifices of pagans are offered to demons, not to you and I should never be a participant with demons. *²¹*Lord, keep me ever vigilant that I cannot drink of your cup, or have a part in your table and do the same with demons. *²²*May I never arouse your jealousy, or suppose that I am stronger than you. *²³*Remind me often I pray, that even though everything is "permissible", not everything is beneficial or constructive. *²⁴*Guide me Master to not seek my own good, but the good of others.

*31-33*Encourage me O' God in whatever I do, to do it all for your glory and to never cause anyone to stumble, but rather try to please everybody in every way, for I should be seeking the good of many instead my own good, so that they may be saved.

11/ Compel me Jesus to be an example to others, as I follow your example. *2*I pray that you train me to remember in everything I do, to hold to the teachings that were passed on to me.

*3 & 11*Help me to fully realize that you are the head of every man and in you, a woman is not independent of man, nor is man independent of woman. *12*For as woman came from man, so also man is born of woman, but everything comes from you Father God.

*23-24*Lord Jesus I pray that you indelibly write on my heart that on the night you were betrayed, you took bread and when you had given thanks, you broke it and said, "This is my body, which is for you; do this in remembrance of me." *25*In the same way, after supper you took the cup, saying, "This cup is the new covenant in my blood; do this, whenever you drink it, in remembrance of me." *26*Let me never forget that whenever I eat this bread and drink of this cup, I am proclaiming your death until you return. *27*Therefore, if I eat the bread or drink of your cup in an unworthy manner, I will be guilty of sinning against your body and blood. *28-29*Remind me Lord that I should examine myself before I eat of the bread and drink of the cup, because if I should eat and drink without recognizing your body, I bring judgment on myself. *30*That is why many are weak and sick, as well as a number who have fallen asleep.

12/Father, keep me from being ignorant about spiritual gifts. *2*I know that when I was a pagan, somehow or other I was influenced and led astray. *3*Master because of that, I ask that you cause me to take into account that no one who is speaking by your Holy Spirit ever says, "Jesus be cursed," nor can they say, "Jesus is Lord," except by that same Holy Spirit. *4-6*Give me I pray, a true understanding that there are different kinds of gifts, services and workings, but you are the same God who works all of them in all men. [7]I ask that you illuminate for me how each one of the manifestations of your Spirit is given for the common good. [8-10]Teach me to recognize that you give one the message of wisdom, to another the message of knowledge, to another faith, to another gifts of healing, to another miraculous powers, to another prophecy, to another distinguishing between spirits, to another speaking in different kinds of tongues, and to still another the interpretation of tongues. [11]All these are the work of one and the same Spirit, and you give them to each one as you determine.

[12]Lord Jesus, I realize that the body is a unit, which it is made up of many parts; and though all its parts are many, they form one body and so it is with you and the church. [13]Keep me conscious of the fact that we were all baptized by the one Holy Spirit into one body and we were all given the one Spirit to drink. [14-16]Since the body is not made up of one part but of many, let me consider that if the foot should say, "Because I am not a hand, I do not belong to the body," or if the ear should say, "Because I am not an eye, I do not belong to the body," they would not for that reason cease to be part of the body.

[17]Guide me I pray to recognize that if the whole body were an eye, where would the sense of hearing be or if the whole body were an ear, where would the sense of smell be? [18]Praise be to you Father God that you have in fact arranged the parts in the body, every one of them, just as you wanted them to be.

[21]Give me the spiritual revelation to recognize that the eye cannot say to the hand, nor can the head say to the feet, "I don't need you!" [22-25]On the contrary, those parts of the body that seem to be weaker are indispensable; likewise the parts that we think are less honorable, we treat with special honor and the parts that are not presentable are treated with special modesty, while our presentable parts need no special treatment. How wise you are Master that you have combined the members of the body and have given greater honor to the parts that lacked it, so that there should be no division in the body, but rather its

parts should have equal concern for each other. ²⁶Keep me aware that if one part suffers, every part suffers with it; if one part is honored, every part rejoices with it.

²⁷Thank you Jesus that we are your body and each of us are a part of it. ²⁸Teach me to recognize that in your church you have appointed first of all apostles, second prophets, third teachers, then workers of miracles, also those having gifts of healing, those able to help others, those with gifts of administration, and those speaking in different kinds of tongues. ²⁹⁻³¹I pray that you keep it clear in my mind that not everyone is an apostle, or a prophet, or a teacher, nor do all work miracles, or have gifts of healing, nor does everyone speak in tongues or interpret, but rather we should eagerly desire the greater gifts and you will show us the most excellent way.

13¹Lord Jesus, help me truly understand that even if I speak in the tongues of men and of angels, but have not love, I am only a resounding gong or a clanging cymbal. ²If I have the gift of prophecy and can fathom all mysteries and all knowledge, and if I have a faith that can move mountains, but have not love, I am nothing. ³If I give all I possess to the poor and surrender my body to the flames, but have not love, I gain nothing.

⁴Father, I pray that you open my heart to understand that love is patient and kind; it is not envious, nor is it boastful or proud. ⁵It is not rude, it is not self-seeking, it is not easily angered and it keeps no record of wrongs. ⁶ Help me to recognize that love does not delight in evil but rejoices with the truth. ⁷It always protects, always trusts, always hopes and always perseveres.

⁸I pray to grasp the truth that where there are prophecies, they will cease; where there are tongues, they will be stilled; where there is knowledge, it will pass away, but love will never fail. ⁹⁻¹⁰For we know in part and we prophesy in part, but when perfection comes, the imperfect disappears. ¹¹When I was a child, I talked like a child; I thought like a

child, I reasoned like a child, but when I became an adult, I put childish ways behind me.

*12*Master, I know that now I see but a poor reflection as in a mirror, but one day I shall see you face to face. Now I know in part; then I shall know fully, even as I am fully known. *13*Bless you my King because these three remain: faith, hope and love, but the greatest of these is love!

14/Father God encourage me to follow the way of love and eagerly desire spiritual gifts, especially the gift of prophecy. *3*For everyone who prophesies speaks to men for their strengthening, encouragement and comfort. *12*Compel me I pray to be eager to use my spiritual gifts and to try to excel in gifts that build up the church. *20*I pray that you teach me to think like an adult, not a child, but in regard to evil to be an infant.

*26*Remind me often, that when the church comes together that we should have a hymn, or a word of instruction, or a revelation, a tongue or an interpretation and all of these must be done for the strengthening of the church. *32-33*Give me the wisdom to understand that the spirits of prophets are subject to the control of prophets, for you O' God are not a God of disorder but of peace.

15/Lord Jesus, I want you to remind me daily of the gospel that was preached to me, which I received and on which I have taken my stand. *2*Cause me to realize that it is by that gospel I am saved, if I hold firmly to the word that was preached to me; otherwise, I have believed in vain. *3-5*Help me Jesus to discover that what I received and should pass on to others as of first importance is: that you died for our sins according to the Scriptures, that you were buried and that you were raised on the third day according to the Scriptures.

*19-20*Father I recognize that if only for this life I have hope in Christ I should be pitied more than all men, but Hallelujah, Jesus has indeed been raised from the dead, the first fruits of those who have fallen asleep! *21*Encourage me with the truth that since death came through a man, the resurrection of the dead comes also through a man. *22-23*Because as in Adam all die, so in Christ all will be made alive, but each in his own turn: Christ, the first fruits; then, when he comes, those who belong to him. [24]Praise you God my Father for in the end, Jesus will hand over the kingdom to you after he has destroyed all dominion, authority and power. [25-26]For he must reign until he has put all his enemies under his feet, the last of which is death.

[33]I pray Master to never be misled and recognize that: "Bad company corrupts good character." [34]I also call upon you to encourage me to keep my senses as I ought and to not sin, nor be ignorant about you. [51-52]Cause me Lord to keep foremost in my mind the mystery that we will not all sleep, but we will all be changed in a flash, in the twinkling of an eye, at the last trumpet. Then the dead will be raised imperishable, and we will be changed, because the perishable must clothe itself with the imperishable and the mortal with immortality.

[54]Praise you Mighty God for when that happens the saying that is written will come true: "Death has been swallowed up in victory." [56-57]Lord I recognize that the sting of death is sin, and the power of sin is the law, but thanks to you Jesus I will have the victory. [58]Strengthen me therefore to stand firm letting nothing move me and to always give myself fully to your work, because I know it is never in vain.

16[1-2]Keep me mindful about the importance of the collection for your people and how on the first day of every week, I should set aside a sum of money in keeping with my income. [13]Keep me on my guard so I can stand firm in the faith and be a strong person of courage. [14&16]Urge me Master to do everything in love and to submit to those who join in the work and labor at it.

REFLECTIONS

_____
_____
_____
_____
_____
_____
_____
_____
_____
_____
_____
_____
_____
_____
_____
_____
_____
_____
_____
_____
_____
_____
_____
_____
_____
_____
_____
_____
_____
_____
_____

The Book of 2nd Corinthians

1 *³*I praise you my Father, because you are the God of all compassion and comfort. *⁴*Thank you for comforting me in all my troubles, so that I can comfort those in any trouble with the same comfort I have received from you. *⁵*Jesus, let me never forget that just as your sufferings flow over into my life, so also through you, my comfort should overflow.

*⁷*I am grateful that my hope is firm, because I know that just as I share in your sufferings, I will also share in your comfort. *¹⁰⁻¹¹*I acknowledge the truth that you have delivered me from peril and will continue to deliver me as I set my hope on you. Master, I give you thanks for the gracious favor granted to me in answer to my prayers. *¹²*Lord, I pray that you keep me conscious of how I conduct myself in the world, especially in my relations with others. Show me how to do it not according to worldly wisdom, but with holiness and sincerity in accordance with your grace.

*¹⁷*Teach me I pray to not make my plans lightly or in a worldly manner so that in the same breath I say, "Yes, yes" and "No, no". *¹⁸⁻¹⁹*Help me to see that your message is not "Yes" and "No", but in you it has always been "Yes." *²⁰*For no matter how many promises you make Mighty God, they are "Yes" in Jesus and so through him the "Amen" can be spoken by me to your glory. *²¹⁻²²*Thank you my King because it is you who makes me stand firm in Christ. I worship you because you anointed me, set your seal of ownership on me and put your Spirit in my hearts as a deposit, guaranteeing what is to come.

3 *²*Help me I pray, to grasp that I am your letter, written on the heart, known and read by everyone *³* Cause me to realize that I am the result of your ministry Jesus, written not with ink, but with the Spirit of the living God, not on tablets of stone, but on the tablet of my heart.

⁴ Thank you Jesus for the confidence that is mine through you. *⁵⁻⁶*I know Father that I am not competent in my own ability to claim anything for myself, but my competence comes from you because you have made me a minister of a new covenant, not of the letter, but of the Spirit; for the letter kills, but the Spirit gives life.

*12*Therefore, since I have such a hope, encourage me Lord to be very bold. *13*Help me realize that I am not like Moses, who would put a veil over his face to keep the Israelites from gazing at it while the radiance was fading away. *14&16*Let me see that their minds were made dull, for to this day the same veil remains when the old covenant is read. It has not been removed, because only in you Jesus is it taken away, because whenever anyone turns to you, the veil is taken away. *17*Encourage me Lord with the truth that you are Spirit and where your Spirit is, there is freedom. *18*Teach me I pray to reflect your glory with an unveiled face and be transformed into your likeness with ever-increasing glory.

4*1*Master, since it is through your mercy that I have this ministry, I will not lose heart. *2-3*Instead, I will renounce secret and shameful ways. I will never use deception, nor will I distort your word. On the contrary, I will set forth the truth plainly to every man's conscience in your sight and if the gospel is veiled, it is veiled to those who are perishing. *4*I pray Jesus that you help me realize that the god of this age has blinded the minds of unbelievers, so that they cannot see the light of the gospel and your glory. *6*Let me not forget O' God that you have said, "Let light shine out of darkness," and that your light will shine in my heart to give me the light of the knowledge of your glory in the face of Christ.

*7*Lord, may I always bear in mind that I have your treasure in this jar of clay to show that this all-surpassing power is from you and not of myself. *8-9*Encourage me with the truth that if I am hard pressed on every side; I will not be crushed, if I am perplexed; I should not despair, if I am persecuted; I will not be abandoned, if I am struck down; I will not be destroyed. *10*Jesus, open my spiritual eyes to see that I always carry around in my body your death, so that your life may also be revealed in my mortal body.

*13-14*Master, it is written: "I believed; therefore I have spoken" and it is with that same spirit of faith I believe and will therefore speak, because

I know that not only did you raise my Lord Jesus from the dead, but you will also raise me with him and I will be presented in your presence. [15]Father God, may I always be aware that this benefit is given to me so that your grace will reach more people and cause thanksgiving to overflow for your glory.

[16-17] I call upon you to strengthen me in my inner man to never lose heart. Allow me to see that even though outwardly I may be wasting away, inwardly I am being renewed day by day and that my light and momentary troubles are achieving eternal glory that far outweighs them all. [18]I pray that you help me to fix my eyes not on what is seen, but on what is unseen, because what is seen is temporary, but what is unseen is eternal.

5[1]I worship you Lord because I know that if the earthly tent I live in is destroyed, I have a building from you that is an eternal house in heaven, not built by human hands. [2-3]In the meantime however I groan, longing to be clothed with my heavenly dwelling, because when I am clothed, I will not be found naked. [4]For while I am in this tent, I groan and am burdened, because I do not wish to be unclothed, but to be clothed with my heavenly dwelling, so that what is mortal may be swallowed up by life.

[5-7]You deserve my adoration Father God because it is you who made me for this very purpose and have given me your Spirit as a deposit, guaranteeing what is to come; therefore I will always be confident. Keep me aware that as long as I am at home in the body I am away from you Lord and that I must live by faith, not by sight.

[8-9]Heavenly Father, I would prefer to be away from the body and be at home with you, however I will make it my goal to please you, whether I am at home in the body or away from it. [10]Keep me aware Jesus that I must appear before your judgment seat, so that I may receive what is due me for the things I've done while in the body, whether good or bad.

*11*Lord, since I know what it is to fear you, I will try to persuade men. *14-15*Your love compels me, because I am fully convinced that you died for all of us, therefore we all also died and since you died for all, those that live should no longer live for themselves, but for you who died for us and was raised again. *16*Teach me to no longer regard anyone from a worldly point of view, even though I at one time regarded you in that way, I certainly do so no longer. *17*Thank you Jesus because since I am in you, I am a new creation; the old has gone, the new has come! *18*I glorify you Father for the reason that all of this is from you, the one who reconciled me through Christ and gave me the ministry of reconciliation. *19*How marvelous it is that you reconciled me to yourself in Jesus, not counting my sins against me and you have committed to me the message of reconciliation. *20*Therefore I am one of your ambassadors and it is as though you are making your appeal through me. *21*Merciful Father, you made Him who had no sin to be sin for me, so that in him I might become the righteousness from you.

6*1-2*As one of your workers Father, urge me I pray to never receive grace in vain because you have said, "In the time of my favor I heard you, and in the day of salvation I helped you." Help me to recognize that, now is the time of your favor and now is the day of salvation. *3*I also pray that I would never put a stumbling block in anyone's path, so that the ministry will not be discredited. *14* Master, I call upon you to remind me often to not become yoked together with unbelievers, because righteousness and wickedness have nothing in common, nor does light have fellowship with darkness. *15-17*Show me the truth that there can never be harmony between Christ and Belial and that there is nothing in common between a believer and an unbeliever anymore than there is agreement between your temple O' God and the temple of idols. Let me always remember that we are your temple and you have said: "I will live with them and walk among them, and I will be their God, and they will be my people. Therefore come out from them and be separate. Touch no unclean thing," *18*Bless you Lord, because you have promised that you will be a Father to us and we will be your sons and daughters and you will receive us.

REFLECTIONS

7¹Heavenly Father, because you have made these promises, I pray that you help me purify myself from everything that contaminates body and spirit, while perfecting holiness out of reverence for you.

9⁶Master, I pray that you help me to always remember that whoever sows sparingly will also reap sparingly, and whoever sows generously will also reap generously. ⁷Teach me to give what I have decided in my heart to give, not reluctantly or under compulsion, because you love a cheerful giver. ⁸I honor you Lord for you are able to make all grace abound to me, so that in all things at all times, having all that I need, I will abound in every good work. ⁹Cause me I pray to bear in mind that it is written: "He has scattered abroad his gifts to the poor; his righteousness endures forever." ¹⁰I know that since you are the one who supplies seed to the sower and bread for food, that you will also supply and increase my store of seed, as well as enlarging the harvest of my righteousness.

¹¹You have made me rich in every way so that I can be generous on every occasion, and through my generosity it will result in thanksgiving to you my King. ¹²I call upon you, Heavenly Father, to keep me aware that the service that I perform; is a supply to the needs of your people and is an overflowing expression of thanks to you. ¹³Make my spiritual vision clear to recognize that the service by which I prove myself, will cause men to praise you for the obedience that accompanies my confession of the gospel and for my generosity in sharing with everyone else. ¹⁵Thank you Lord for this indescribable gift!

10³My Father God, keep me keenly aware that even though I live in the world, I should not wage war as the world does. ⁴The weapons I should fight with are not the weapons of the world, on the contrary; they have divine power to demolish strongholds. ⁵Keep me aware that I should demolish every argument and pretension that sets itself up against the knowledge of you, as well as taking captive every thought to make it obedient to Christ.

*12*Lord may I never dare to classify or compare myself with those who commend themselves because when they measure and compare themselves with themselves, they are not wise.

*15-16*My prayer is that as my faith continues to grow; my area of activity will greatly expand, so that I can share the gospel with others. *17*Help me to realize that if there is to be any boasting, it should be about you. *18*For it is not the one who commends himself who is approved, but the one whom you, the God of Heaven commends.

11 *13*Lord, I also pray that you keep me alert and watchful for men that are false apostles and deceitful workmen that masquerade as your apostles. *14*Help me to realize that it is no wonder, since Satan himself masquerades as an angel of light, that his servants then would masquerade as servants of righteousness. Let me not forget that their end will be what their actions deserve.

13 *5-6*Master, encourage me to examine myself to see whether I am in the faith and to test myself. I pray Jesus that you open my understanding to realize that you are in me unless, of course, I fail the test and I trust that you will keep me from failing the test.

*7*Now I pray that I will not do anything wrong, not so that people will see that I have stood the test, but so that I will do what is right. *8*Holy Spirit, compel me to never do anything against the truth, but rather to do things for the truth. *9-10*Lord, whenever I am weak; strengthen me. My prayer is for perfection so that I can build others up, not tear them down. *11*Finally, teach me to aim for perfection and be single minded so that your peace will be with me. *14*May your grace Lord Jesus, and your love O' God, as well as your fellowship Holy Spirit, be always with me.

REFLECTIONS

The Book of Galatians

1 *3*Thank you, Father God, for the grace and peace you have given to me. *4&5*Praise you, Jesus, for giving yourself for my sins to rescue me from this present evil age, according to the will of God, to whom be glory for ever and ever.

*10*I pray that you keep me aware that I should not be trying to win the approval of men, but instead always be your servant and try to please you. *11- 12*Jesus, I ask that you keep me ever attentive to the fact that the gospel is not something that man made up, nor was I taught it; instead I received it by revelation from you through the preaching of the Scripture *15- 16*Blessed be your name Mighty God, because you set me apart from birth, called me by your grace and were pleased to reveal your Son in me so that I might proclaim him among mankind.

2 *16*Keep me ever aware that a man is not justified by observing the law, but by faith in you Jesus because: no one will be justified by observing the law. *19*For through the law I died to the law so that I might live for you O' God. *20*Thank you Heavenly Father that I have been crucified with Christ and I no longer live, but Christ lives in me. Let me never forget my Savior, that the life I live in the body, I live by faith in you, the Son of God, who loved me and gave himself for me. *21*I pray that you guide me to remain attentive and not set aside your grace, for if righteousness could be gained through the law, you died for nothing!

3 *2*Let me never forget, my Redeemer, that I did not receive the Spirit by observing the law, but by believing what I heard. *3*Keep me focused I pray, so I will not be foolish enough as to believe that after beginning with the Spirit, I would try to attain my goal by human effort. *5* Thank you, that you give me your Spirit and work miracles for me, not because I observe the law, but because I believe what I have heard from you.

*6 & 7*Help me to grasp that because Abraham believed you God, it was credited to him as righteousness and since I believe, I am a child of Abraham. *9*Thank you that in view of the fact that I have faith: I am blessed along with Abraham, the man of faith. *11*Master let it always be clear to me that no one is justified before you by the law, because; "The righteous will live by faith." *13*Bless you Jesus because you redeemed me from the curse of the law by becoming a curse for me, for it is written: "Cursed is everyone who is hung on a tree."

*14*I am so grateful, my Great Shepard, that you redeemed me in order that the blessing given to Abraham might come to me, so that by faith I now receive the promise of the Spirit. *19*Help me, I pray, to come to terms with the truth that the purpose of the law being added was because of transgressions. That is until you, Jesus, "the Seed" to whom the promise referred had come.

*22*Help me to comprehend that the Scriptures declare that I was a prisoner of sin and what was promised is given through faith in Jesus Christ to me as a believer. *23*Give me the clarity of thought to realize that before my faith came, I was held prisoner by the law, locked up until faith should be revealed. *24 & 25*Keep me mindful of the truth that; the law was put in charge to lead me to you Jesus, so that I might be justified by faith. Oh, how thankful I am now that faith has come, I am no longer under the supervision of the law.

4 *4 & 5*Thank you merciful God that when the time had fully come, you sent your Son, born of a woman, born under law, to redeem those under law, so that we might receive the full rights of sons. *6*Let me always recognize that I am your son and that you sent the Spirit of your son Jesus into my heart, the Spirit who calls out, *"Abba,* Father." *7* Praise you merciful God that I am no longer a slave, but a son; and since I am a son, you have made me also an heir. *8 & 9*Formerly, when I did not know you Father God, I was a slave to those who by nature are not gods, but now that I know you, or rather are known by you, keep me I pray from ever turning back to those weak and miserable principles because I do not wish to be enslaved by them all over again.

5/Since it is for freedom that you set me free Jesus; remind me to stand firm and not let myself be burdened again by a yoke of slavery. ⁶For in you the only thing that counts is faith expressing itself through love. ¹⁰Lord keep me confident to take no other view.

¹³Since you called me to be free Heavenly Father, never let me use my freedom to indulge my sinful nature, but rather, serve others in the Spirit of love. ¹⁴Let me never forget that the entire law is summed up in a single command: "Love your neighbor as yourself." ¹⁶Strengthen me I pray to live by the Spirit, so I will not gratify the desires of the sinful nature. ^{17 & 18}For the sinful nature desires what is contrary to the Spirit and the Spirit desires what is contrary to the sinful nature. Help me then Master, to realize that they are in conflict with each other; so that I do not do what I want, but if I am led by your Spirit, I am not under law.

¹⁹Keep me vigilant to recognize that the acts of the sinful nature are obvious: sexual immorality, impurity and debauchery; ²⁰idolatry and witchcraft; hatred, discord, jealousy, fits of rage, selfish ambition, dissensions, factions ²¹and envy; drunkenness, orgies, and the like. Keep me in remembrance that I have been warned, that those who live like this will not inherit the kingdom of God. ²²Let me consider daily that the fruit of the Spirit is love, joy, peace, patience, kindness, goodness, faithfulness, ²³gentleness and self-control. Against such things there is no law. ²⁴Because I belong to you Christ Jesus, I will crucify my sinful nature with its passions and desires! ²⁵Since I live by the Spirit, let me keep in step with the Spirit. ²⁶Master, never let me become conceited, provoking and envying others.

6/Father, if I catch someone in a sin, let me be spiritual and restore them gently, but watch myself lest I also be tempted. ²Remind me to carry other's burdens, and in this way I will fulfill the law of Christ. ³Let me not forget that if I think I am something when I am nothing, I deceive myself.

*4 & 5*Give me the wisdom to test my own actions so I can take pride in myself, without comparing myself to someone else, never forgetting that I should carry my own load.

*7*Master, do not let me be deceived, for you cannot be mocked; I will reap what I sow. *8*If I sow to please my sinful nature, from that nature I will reap destruction, but if I sow to please the Spirit, from the Spirit I will reap eternal life. *9*I pray for strength to never become weary in doing good, for at the proper time I will reap a harvest if I do not give up. *10*Therefore Father God, as I have opportunity, let me do good to all people, especially to those who belong to the family of believers. *14*May I never boast in anything except in the cross of my Lord Jesus Christ, through which the world has been crucified to me, and I to the world.

REFLECTIONS

_____

_____

_____

_____

_____

_____

_____

_____

_____

_____

_____

_____

_____

The Book of Ephesians

1 *³*Father of my Lord Jesus Christ, I praise you, for you have blessed me in the heavenly realms with every spiritual blessing. *⁴, ⁵ & ⁶*Thank you, Father, for choosing me (in Jesus) before the creation of the world to be holy and blameless in your sight. I give you glory my King, because in love you predestined me to be adopted as one of your sons through Jesus Christ, in accordance with your pleasure, your will and to the praise of your glorious grace, which you have freely given to me in the One whom you love.

*⁷*I am grateful Jesus; that I have redemption through your blood, as well as the forgiveness of my sins in accordance with the riches of God's grace. *⁸*I am even more grateful Father, that you lavished it on me with all wisdom and understanding. *⁹*I praise you Father God for making known to me the mystery of your will according to your good pleasure, which you purposed in Christ. *¹⁰*I am indebted to you because you put it into effect when the times will have reached their fulfillment, to bring all things in heaven and on earth together under one head, even Christ. *¹³*I am so blessed that you included me in Christ when I heard and believed the word of truth, the gospel of my salvation. I thank you further that I was marked in Jesus with a seal, the promised Holy Spirit; *¹⁴*who is the deposit guaranteeing my inheritance until my redemption as one of your possessions.

*¹⁷*I ask you glorious Father, to give me the Spirit of wisdom and revelation, so that I may know you better. *¹⁸, ¹⁹, ²⁰ & ²¹*I pray also that the eyes of my heart may be enlightened in order that I may know the hope to which you have called me which is; the riches of your glorious inheritance in the saints and your incomparable great power for me as a believer. This power is like the working of your mighty strength, which you exerted in Christ when you raised him from the dead and seated him at your right hand in the heavenly realms, far above all rule and authority, power and dominion, and every title that can be given; not only in the present age, but also in the one to come. *²² & ²³*Praise you O God, that you placed all things under Jesus' feet and appointed him to be head over everything for the church, which is his body, the fullness of him who fills everything in every way.

2 *1 & 2*As for me, I was dead in my transgressions and sins, in which I used to live when I followed the ways of this world and the ruler of the kingdom of the air, whose spirit is now at work in those who are disobedient. *3*I also lived among them at one time, gratifying the cravings of my sinful nature by following its desires and thoughts. Like the rest, I was by nature, an object of wrath. *4,5*I praise you my Father, because of your great love for me and the richness your mercy. I praise you, for you made me alive with Christ even when I was dead in transgressions; it is by grace that I have been saved.

*6 & 7*Bless you mighty God, for raising me up with Christ and seating me with him spiritually in the heavenly realms, in order that in the coming ages you may show the incomparable riches of your grace.

*8, 9*For it is by grace that I have been saved, through faith, and this is not of myself, it is a gift from you O God, it is not by works, so that no one can boast. *10*Let me never forget my Master, that I am your workmanship, created in Christ Jesus to do good works, which you prepared in advance for me to do.

*12*Help me to remember that at one time I was separate from you Jesus. I was excluded from the citizenship in Israel and a foreigner to the covenants of the promise. I was without hope and without God my Father in the world. *13*But now, in you Christ Jesus even though I was once far away, I have been brought near through your blood.

*14, 15 & 16*For you Jesus are my peace and you have made the two one, as well as destroying the barrier, the dividing wall of hostility, by abolishing in your flesh the law with its commandments and regulations. Help me to fully realize that your purpose was to create in yourself one new man out of the two, thus making peace and in your body reconciling both of them to God through the cross, by which you put to death their hostility.

[17] Thank you Jesus, because you came and preached thereby bringing peace to me, as well as to anyone who was far away or near. [18]For through you Jesus, we all have access to the Father by one Spirit. [19] & [20]Consequently, I am no longer a foreigner or an alien, but a fellow citizen with God's people and a member of God's household, built on the foundation of the apostles and prophets, with you my Savior, as the chief cornerstone. [21& 22]I stand amazed Mighty God, that in Jesus the whole building is joined together and rises to become a holy temple in you and also in Jesus; I too, along with other saints, am being built together to become a dwelling in which you O God live by your Spirit.

3[7]Master, I realize that I am indebted to this gospel by your gift of grace which you gave me through the working of your power. [8 & 9]Although I feel like the least of all your people, this grace you have given me causes in me the desire to share your unsearchable riches and to make plain to everyone the mystery, which for ages past was kept hidden in you O God, who created all things. [10 & 11] Illuminate for me Father the truth that your intent was and is: that your manifold wisdom should be made known to the rulers and authorities in the heavenly realms through the church, according to your eternal purpose which you accomplished in Christ Jesus my Lord. [12]I thank you Jesus, that through faith in you I may approach God with freedom and confidence.

[14 & 15] For this reason I kneel before you Father, from whom the whole family in heaven and on earth derives its name. [16, 17 & 18]I pray that out of your glorious riches you may strengthen me with power through your Spirit in my inner being, so that Christ may dwell in my heart through faith. I pray that being rooted and established in love, I may have power, together with all the saints, to grasp how wide and long and high and deep is the love of Christ. [19]I ask of you Father God, to know this love that surpasses knowledge so that I may be filled to the measure of all the fullness of you.

[20]My mouth is filled with praise for you Mighty God, because you are able to do immeasurably more than all I ask or imagine, according to your power that is at work within me.

4 *¹*As a prisoner for you Lord, urge me to live a life worthy of the calling I have received. *²*Help me Father, to be completely humble, gentle and patient, as well as bearing with others in love. *³* Give to me the right attitude Master, to make every effort to keep the unity of the Spirit through the bond of peace. *⁴,⁵ & ⁶*Let me always remember that there is one body, one Spirit, one hope, one Lord, one faith and one baptism; one God and Father of all, who is over all, through all and in all of us. *⁷,⁸*Keep me mindful my King, that grace has been given to me as Christ apportioned it and that is why it says: "When he ascended on high, he led captives in his train and gave gifts to men."

*¹¹, ¹² &¹³*Let me act upon the revelation Father, that you have given some to be apostles, some to be prophets, some to be evangelists, and some to be pastors and teachers, to prepare us (your people) for works of service. Thank you Lord, because you did it so that the body of Christ may be built up until we all become mature, attaining the whole measure of the fullness of Christ, as well as reach unity in the faith and the knowledge of your son Jesus. *¹⁴* Consequently then; I will no longer be an infant, tossed back and forth by the waves, and blown here and there by every wind of teaching, or by the cunning and craftiness of men in their deceitful scheming. *¹⁵*Bless me my Teacher instead, to speak the truth in love, and to grow up into you; the Head, that is, Christ. *¹⁶*Help me to become conscious of the truth; that in you Jesus, the whole body is joined and held together by every supporting ligament and grows by building itself up in love, as each part does its work.

*¹⁷*Lord, strengthen me so that I no longer live as unbelievers do, in the futility of their thinking. *¹⁸*They are darkened in their understanding and separated from the life with you O God, because of the ignorance that is in them due to the hardening of their hearts. *¹⁹*They have lost all sensitivity and have given themselves over to sensuality so as to indulge in every kind of impurity, with a continual lust for more. *²⁰*I, however, did not come to know you, Jesus, that way. *²¹*I heard of you and was taught in you in accordance with the truth that is in you. *²², ²³ & ²⁴*I was taught, with regard to my former way of life; to put off the old self, which is being corrupted by its deceitful desires and to be made new in the attitude of my mind by putting on the new self, created to be like my Father God, in true righteousness and holiness. *²⁵*Therefore my Father, I must put off falsehood and speak truthfully to my neighbor, for we are all members of one body.

*²⁶ & ²⁷*Strengthen me so that when I am angered, I would not sin, nor would I let the sun go down while I am still angry, and never give the devil a foothold. *²⁸*Remind me my Master, that I must work doing something useful with my own hands, that I may have something to share with those in need.

*²⁹*Sanctify me O Holy Spirit, so that no unwholesome talk would come out of my mouth, but only what is helpful for building others up according to their needs, that it may benefit those who listen. *³⁰*Bless me so that I will not grieve you; Holy Spirit of God, with whom I am sealed for the day of redemption. *³¹*Compel me to; get rid of all bitterness, rage and anger, brawling and slander, along with every form of malice. *³²*Remind me always to be kind and compassionate to others, forgiving others, just as in Christ, you forgave me.

5*¹*As one of your dearly loved children, empower me to be an imitator of you Father God. *²*Bless me to live a life of love, just as Christ loved me and gave himself up for me as a fragrant offering and sacrifice to you O God. *³* Sanctify me so that there is not even a hint of sexual immorality, impurity or of greed in me, because these are improper for God's holy people. *⁴*Cleanse me so that no obscenity, foolish talk or coarse joking would ever come out of my mouth, all of which are out of place; instead let it always be thanksgiving. *⁵*Let me never forget that no immoral, impure or greedy person, has any inheritance in your kingdom Mighty God. *⁶*My Father, keep me attentive so that no one deceives me with empty words, for because of such things; your wrath will come on those who are disobedient. *⁷*Therefore my Master, do not let me be found as a partner with them. *⁸, ⁹ & ¹⁰* Even though I was once darkness, now I am light in you Lord. Strengthen me to live as a child of light; which consists of the fruit of goodness, righteousness and truth and help me to find out what pleases you my King. *¹¹, ¹²* I also pray that you give me the wisdom to have nothing to do with the fruitless deeds of darkness, but rather expose them, since it is shameful even to mention what the disobedient do in secret. *13,14*Help me embrace the truth that; everything exposed by the light becomes visible, for it is light that makes everything visible. This is why it is said: "Wake up, O sleeper, rise from the dead, and Christ will shine on you."

*15,16*Stimulate me Holy Spirit, to be very careful then how I live; not as unwise, but as wise and to make the most of every opportunity, because the days are evil. *17*Therefore do not let me be foolish, but rather help me understand what your will is. *18*Let me never get drunk on wine, which leads to debauchery, instead let me be filled with the Spirit. *19, 20* I ask that you keep me mindful to speak to others with psalms, hymns and spiritual songs. Let me also sing and make music in my heart to you Lord, always giving thanks to you my God and my Father for everything. *21*Out of reverence for you Jesus, remind me to submit to the brethren.

*22*I pray that wives would submit to their husbands as they would to you, Lord. *23*I pray that they would recognize that the husband is the head of the wife just as Christ is the head of the church, his body, of which he is the Savior. *24*Father God, give them the revelation that; as the church submits to Christ, so also should wives submit to their husbands in everything.

*25, 26, 27*Likewise, I call upon you to urge husbands to love their wives, just as Christ loved the church and gave himself up for her. Jesus help them; as well as I, realize that you did this for the church to make her holy, cleansing her by the washing with water through the word, and to present her to himself as a radiant church, without stain or wrinkle or any other blemish, but holy and blameless.

*28*In this same way my Master, teach husbands to love their wives as their own bodies. He who loves his wife loves himself. *29, 30*After all, no one ever hated his own body, but he feeds and cares for it, just as you Jesus do the church; for we are members of your body. *31*Mighty God, let your church always be mindful of the truth that says "For this reason a man will leave his father and mother and be united to his wife, and the two will become one flesh." *32*This is a profound mystery about Christ and the church. *33*However, I pray earnestly that accordingly may men love their wives as themselves, and wives respect their husband.

6*1*Heavenly Father, I pray for children everywhere to obey their parents, for this is right. *2, 3*You have surely and plainly stated "Honor your father and mother"; which is the first commandment you gave with the promise; "that it may go well with you and that you may enjoy long life on the earth." *4*I pray specifically for fathers, that they would not exasperate their children, but instead, bring them up in the training and instruction of you my Lord.

*5*As a slave would; remind me to obey my earthly masters just as I would obey you Jesus, with respect, fear and with sincerity of heart,. *6*Uphold me with your strength to obey them; not only to win their favor when their eye is on me, but like I was your slave Lord, doing your will O' God from my heart. *7&8*Encourage me Lord to serve wholeheartedly, as if I were serving you, not men, because I know that as the righteous Judge; you will reward everyone for whatever good they do. *9*Also, when I am in a place of authority encourage me to treat others under me in the same way as you would and not threaten them, since I know that he who is both their Master and mine is in heaven and there is no favoritism with you.

*10*Finally, I pray to be strong in you O' Lord and in your mighty power. *11*Remind me daily to put on your full armor Mighty God, so that I can take my stand against the devil's schemes. *12* Help me to realize that my struggle is not against flesh and blood, but against the rulers, the authorities, and the powers of this dark world, as well as the spiritual forces of evil in the heavenly realms. *13*Therefore, remind me daily to put on your full armor Father God, so that when the day of evil comes; I may be able to stand my ground and after I have done everything, to then make my stand. *14*Encourage me my King, to stand firm then, with the belt of truth buckled around my waist and the breastplate of righteousness in place. ¹⁵Keep my feet fitted with the readiness that comes from the gospel of peace. ¹⁶In addition to all this, rouse me to take up the shield of faith, with which I can extinguish all the flaming arrows of the evil one.

¹⁷Help me always remember to put on the helmet of salvation and use the sword of the Spirit, which is your word O' God. ¹⁸Give me the faithfulness to pray in the Spirit on all occasions with all kinds of prayers and requests. With this in mind, keep me alert and always encourage me to keep on praying for all the saints. ¹⁹ & ²⁰I also pray; that whenever I open my mouth, words may be given to me by you my Father; so that I will fearlessly make known the mystery of the gospel, for which I am an ambassador.

REFLECTIONS

_____

_____

_____

_____

_____

_____

_____

_____

_____

_____

_____

_____

_____

_____

_____

_____

The Book of Philippians

1 *3-5* I thank you Mighty God every time in all my prayers because of my partnership in the gospel from the first day until now. *6*Father, I am confident of this, that since you began a good work in me that you will carry it on to completion until the day of Christ Jesus.

*9*Lord and Father this is my prayer: that my love for you may abound more and more in knowledge and depth of insight, *10*so that I may be able to discern what is best and that I may be pure and blameless until the day of Christ, *11*I pray to be filled with the fruit of righteousness that comes through Jesus Christ for your glory and praise O God.

*18*Father, remind me to always rejoice *19*in knowing that through prayer and the help given by the Spirit of Jesus Christ, that whatever happens to me will turn out for my deliverance. *20*I pray that I will in no way be ashamed, but will have sufficient courage so that Jesus will be exalted in my body, whether by life or by death. *21*For to me, to live is Christ and to die is gain. *27*Whatever happens Lord, help me to conduct myself in a manner worthy of the gospel of Christ and to stand firm with other Christians in one spirit, contending as one man for the faith of the gospel *28*without being frightened in any way by those who oppose us. *29*Father, help me to realize that it has been granted to us on behalf of Christ, not only to believe on him, but also to suffer for him.

2 *1*Jesus, since I have encouragement from being united with you and the comfort from your love, as well as fellowship with the Spirit including tenderness and compassion, *2* let me make your joy complete by being like-minded, having the same love, being one with you in spirit and purpose. *3*Lord let me not do anything out of selfish ambition or vain conceit, but in humility considering others better than myself. *4*Keep me in remembrance to not only look out for my own interests, but also the interests of others. *5*Help my attitude to be the same as yours Christ Jesus; to make nothing of myself, to take on the very nature of a servant, *8*to humble myself and become obedient even unto death.

⁹Therefore, because of your attitude Jesus; our Father God exalted you to the highest place and gave you the name that is above every name, ¹⁰that at that name every knee should bow, in heaven and on earth and under the earth, ¹¹and every tongue confess that you Jesus; are Lord, to the glory of God the Father.

¹²Father, grant me wisdom and strength to continue working out my salvation with fear and trembling, ¹³since it is you O God who works in me to will and to act according to your good purpose. ¹⁴Help me to do everything without complaining or arguing, ¹⁵so that I may become blameless and pure, a child of God without fault in a crooked and depraved generation, in which I can shine like a star in the universe ¹⁶as I hold out the word of life.

3¹Master, let me always rejoice in you, and put no confidence in the flesh, ⁷because whatever was to my profit I now consider loss for the sake of Christ. ⁸What is more; I consider everything a loss compared to the surpassing greatness of knowing you Jesus. I consider them rubbish, that I may gain you Lord ⁹and be found in you, not having a righteousness of my own that comes from the law, but that which is through faith in you--the righteousness that comes from God and is by faith. ¹⁰⁻¹¹I want to know you Jesus and the power of your resurrection, the fellowship of sharing in your sufferings and become like you in your death, so that I will attain the resurrection from the dead. ¹²I know that I have not already obtained all this, nor have I already been made perfect, but I want you to strengthen me to press on, to take hold of that for which you Jesus took hold of me. ¹³I do not consider myself yet to have taken hold of it, but one thing I want to do for you is: to forget what is behind, strain toward what is ahead and ¹⁴ press on toward the goal, to win the prize for which you Heavenly Father have called me heavenward in Christ Jesus.

¹⁶Father, bless me to live up to what I have already attained ²⁰and since my citizenship is in heaven; I will eagerly await my Savior from there, the Lord Jesus Christ, ²¹who, by the power that enables him to bring

everything under his control, will transform my lowly body so that it will be like his glorious body.

4 *4*Help me; Heavenly Father to always rejoice in you and *5*let my gentleness be evident to all. Since you are near Jesus; *6*do not let me be anxious about anything, but in everything, by prayer, petition and thanksgiving, present my requests to the God of Heaven. *7*Keep me mindful of your peace O God, which transcends all understanding and that it will guard my heart and my mind in Christ Jesus.

*8*Finally Father, whatever is true, whatever is noble, whatever is right, whatever is pure, whatever is lovely, whatever is admirable, excellent or praiseworthy; guide me to think about such things. *9*Whatever I have learned, seen, received or heard from you or others that are strong in the faith; bless me, to put it into practice, knowing that you; the God of peace will be with me. *11*Remind me Father God, to be content whatever the circumstances, *12*whether in need, or when I have plenty. Help me to learn the secret of being content in any and every situation, whether well fed or hungry, whether living in plenty or in want. *13*I can do everything through you who gives me strength. *19*Thank you Father because you will meet all my needs according to your glorious riches in Christ Jesus. *20*To you my God and Father be glory for ever and ever.

REFLECTIONS

The Book of Colossians

1³I always want to first thank you my Heavenly Father when I pray, ⁴because of my faith in Christ Jesus and for the love you have given me for all the saints. ^{5&6}This faith and love spring from the hope that is stored up for me in heaven and from what I have already heard in the word of truth, the gospel that has come to me. All over the world this gospel is bearing fruit and growing, just as it has been doing in me since the day I heard it and understood your grace in all its truth. ^{7&8}I am thankful that I learned it from dear fellow servants, who are faithful ministers of Christ, who also told me about your love through the Holy Spirit.

⁹For this reason, I will not stop asking you to fill me with the knowledge of your will through all spiritual wisdom and understanding. ¹⁰I pray this in order that I may live a life worthy of you Lord and may please you in every way. I also pray that I would bear fruit in every good work and grow in the knowledge of you my Savior. ¹¹I beseech you to strengthen me with all power according to your glorious might, so that I may have great endurance and patience. ¹² Remind me often my Father, to joyfully give thanks for qualifying me to share in the inheritance of the saints in your kingdom of light. ^{13&14}Thank you for rescuing me from the dominion of darkness and bringing me into the kingdom of your Son whom you love; in Him I have redemption and the forgiveness of sins.

¹⁵Jesus, let me never forget that you are the image of the invisible God, the firstborn over all creation. ¹⁶I give you praise; for by you all things were created in heaven and on earth, visible and invisible. Whether thrones or powers or rulers or authorities; all things were created by you and for you. ¹⁷Blessed be your name Jesus, because you are before all things, and in you all things are held together. ¹⁸You are the head of the body, the church and are the beginning; the firstborn from among the dead, so that in everything you might have the supremacy. ^{19&20}How marvelous Heavenly Father that you were pleased to have all your fullness dwell in Jesus, and through him reconcile to yourself all things,

whether things on earth or things in heaven, by making peace through his blood, shed on the cross.

²¹At one time I was alienated from you Father God and was an enemy in my mind because of my evil behavior. ²²&²³But now, you have reconciled me by Christ's physical body through death to present me holy in your sight, without blemish and free from accusation; if I continue in my faith, established and firm, not moved from the hope held out in the gospel. This is the gospel that I heard and that has been proclaimed to every creature under heaven, and of which I am now a servant.

²⁴ I rejoice in any suffering and I fill up in my flesh what is still lacking regarding your afflictions Jesus, for the sake of your body, which is the church. ²⁵&²⁶I have become its servant by the commission God gave me to present the Word in its fullness, i.e. the mystery that has been kept hidden for ages and generations, but is now disclosed to the saints. ²⁷ Thank you Mighty God, for choosing to make known to me the glorious riches of this mystery, which is Christ in me, the hope of glory.

²⁸ I pledge to proclaim him, admonishing and teaching everyone with all wisdom, so that I may present everyone perfect in Christ. ²⁹To this end I will labor, struggling with all your energy, which so powerfully works in me.

2²Heavenly Father, may my purpose always be to encourage others in their heart and unite them in love, so that they may have the full riches of complete understanding, in order that they, as well as I, may know the mystery of a mighty God, namely Christ. ³In you Jesus are hidden all the treasures of wisdom and knowledge. ⁴&⁵I pray that I would never be deceived by fine-sounding arguments, but rather be orderly and have a firm faith in you

⁶So then, just as I have received you Jesus as my Lord, encourage me to continue to live in you. ⁷May I always be rooted and built up in you, strengthened in the faith as I was taught, and overflowing with thankfulness. ⁸ Inspire me to see to it that no one takes me captive

through hollow and deceptive philosophy, which depends on human tradition and the basic principles of this world rather than on Christ.

9&10Praise you Jesus, for all the fullness of the Deity lives in you in bodily form, and I have been given your fullness. You, my Savior are the head over every power and authority! 11In you I was also circumcised, in the putting off of my sinful nature, not with a circumcision done by the hands of men but with the circumcision done by you the Christ. 12I glorify you Jesus having been buried with you in baptism and raised with you through my faith in the power of God, who raised you from the dead.

13&14 I am so grateful that when I was dead in my sins and in the uncircumcision of my sinful nature, you my King, made me alive with Christ. You forgave me of all my sins, having canceled the written code, with its regulations, that was against me and that stood opposed to me; you took it away, nailing it to the cross. 15I am in awe that having disarmed the powers and authorities, you made a public spectacle of them, triumphing over them by the cross.

16Therefore with your grace, I will never let anyone judge me by what I eat or drink, or with regard to a religious festival, a celebration or a special day. 17These are a shadow of the things that were to come; the reality, however, is found in you Jesus. 18Do not let me ever have anyone disqualify me for the prize by their unspiritual mind or idle notions. 19Help me I pray, to always keep my connection with the Head, from whom the whole body is supported and held together by its ligaments and sinews, grows as you Father God causes it to grow.

20&21Since I died with you my Savoir to the basic principles of this world; keep me mindful that I longer belong to it and therefore do not submit to its rules such as: "Do not handle! Do not taste! Do not touch!" 22 Keep me ever vigilant to realize that these are all destined to perish with use, because they are based on human commands and teachings.

23Let me not be deceived and fully understand that such regulations indeed have an appearance of wisdom, with their self-imposed worship, their false humility and their harsh treatment of the body, but they lack any value in restraining sensual indulgence.

3 *1*Since I have been raised with you Christ Jesus; minister to me to set my hearts on things above, where you are seated at the right hand of God. *2*I ask that you show me the way to set my mind on things above, not on earthly things. *3*Since you died for me Jesus, my life is now hidden with you in a most merciful God. *4*Savior, since you now are my life; when you appear, I also will appear with you in glory. *5*Strengthen me therefore, to put to death whatever belongs to my earthly nature: sexual immorality, impurity, lust, evil desires and greed, which is idolatry. *6*May I remain ever mindful that because of these, your wrath O' God is coming.

*7&8*Even though I used to walk in these ways, in the life I once lived, I now must rid myself of all such things as these: anger, rage, malice, slander, and filthy language from my lips. *9*Master, do not let me lie to others, since I have taken off my old self with its practices. *10* Help me daily to put on the new self, which is being renewed in knowledge and in the image of you, my Creator.

*12*Therefore Heavenly Father, as one of your chosen people, holy and dearly loved, guide me daily to clothe myself with compassion, kindness, humility, gentleness and patience. *13*Remind me Father to bear with others and forgive whatever grievances I may have against them. Lead me to forgive, as you Lord forgave me. *14*Give me the wisdom I pray, to realize that over all these virtues I need to put on love, which binds them all together in perfect unity. *15*I call upon you Jesus, to let your peace rule in my heart, since as a member of the one body; I am called to peace and to be thankful. *16*I ask my Father, to let the words of Christ dwell in me richly as I teach and admonish others with all wisdom and as I sing psalms, hymns and spiritual songs with gratitude in my heart to you o' God. *17*I pray that in whatever I do, whether in word or deed, that I would do it all in your name Lord Jesus, giving thanks to God my Father.

[18]I pray that wives would submit to their husbands, as is fitting in the Lord. [19]I also pray that husbands would love their wives and would never be harsh with them. [20]Further I pray that children would obey their parents in everything, for this pleases you Lord. [21]I make intercession for fathers so that they would not embitter their children and thereby cause them to become discouraged. [22]Since you are my Master, I solicit your wisdom to obey any earthly masters I may have in everything. Help me to do it, not only when their eye is on me and to win their favor, but with sincerity of heart and reverence for you Lord. [23]I pray that whatever I do, cause me to work at it with all my heart, as working for you Lord, not for men. [24]Since I know that I will receive an inheritance from you my King as a reward; it is you that I am serving. [25]Keep me ever mindful that anyone who does wrong will be repaid for their wrong, and there is no favoritism.

4[1]Heavenly Father, remind me often to provide for anyone in my charge what is right and fair, because I too have a Master in heaven. [2]Teach me Lord, to devote myself to prayer, being watchful and thankful. [3&4]I also pray that you mighty God, may open a door for your message, so that I may proclaim the mystery of Christ and that I may proclaim it clearly, as I should. [5]Let me be wise in the way I act toward outsiders, making the most of every opportunity. [6]Bless me so that my conversation may always be full of grace and seasoned with salt; so that I may know how to answer everyone. [12]As one of your servants Christ Jesus; keep me always wrestling in prayer so that I may stand firm in all the will of God, mature and fully assured.

REFLECTIONS

The Book of 1ˢᵗ Thessalonians

1²I want to always thank you first my God, in all of my prayers. ³ Thank you Jesus for your work which produced my faith. Let my labor be prompted by love, and my endurance inspired by my hope in you the Lord Jesus Christ. ⁴Let me never forget that you chose me. ⁵I am persuaded of this because the gospel came to me not simply with words, but also with power, with the Holy Spirit and with deep conviction. ⁶I pray that you strengthen me to become an imitator of you Lord Jesus; in spite of severe suffering. ⁹ & ¹⁰Encourage me to always serve you; the living and true God and to wait for your Son Jesus from heaven, whom you raised from the dead and who will rescue us from the coming wrath.

3⁷Heavenly Father, receive from me my thanks, for in all my distress and persecutions I am continually encouraged because of my faith in you. ⁸For now I really live when I am standing firm in you Lord. ⁹How can I thank you enough in return for all the joy that I have in your presence? ¹²Make my love increase and overflow for everyone else, just as it does for you my King. ¹³Strengthen my heart I pray, so that I will be blameless and holy in your presence when my Lord Jesus comes with all his holy ones.

4¹Show me how to live in order to please you Mighty God; and urge me for the cause of the Lord Jesus to do this more and more. ²For I know what instructions were given to me by the authority of Jesus my Savior. ³Since it is your will O' God that I should be sanctified and I should avoid sexual immorality, I pray that you strengthen me in my inner man. ⁴ & ⁵Help me to learn to control my own body in a way that is holy and honorable, not in passionate lust like the heathen, who do not know you my King. ⁶ & ⁷Teach me to never wrong my brother or take advantage of him since you my Lord will punish me for all such sins. For you Mighty God did not call me to be impure, but to live a holy life. ⁸Therefore, if I reject your instruction it means that I do not reject man but you, who gives me your Holy Spirit.

*9 & 10*Just now Lord I pray that you urge me to continue in brotherly love, for you have taught me to love others and in fact to do so more and more. *11 & 12*Guide me I pray to make it my ambition to lead a quiet life, to mind my own business and to work with my hands, so that my daily life may win the respect of outsiders and so that I will not be dependent on anybody.

13 Remind me often my Father not to be ignorant about those who fall asleep; or to grieve like the rest of men who have no hope. *14*I believe that Jesus died and rose again and so I believe that you O' God will bring with Jesus those who have fallen asleep in him. *15*Thank you Lord that according to your own word, you tell me that we who are still alive and are left until your coming, will certainly not precede those who have fallen asleep. *16*For you Jesus will come down from heaven, with a loud command and with the voice of the archangel, as well as the trumpet call of God, and then the dead in Christ will rise first. *17* After that, we who are still alive and are left will be caught up together with them in the clouds to meet you Lord in the air and so we will be with you my Savior, forever. *18*Thank you my Redeemer for those encouraging words and prompt me often to share them with others.

5*1*Jesus, I pray that you give me peace regarding the times and dates of your return. *2*For I know very well that the day of the Lord will come like a thief in the night. *3 & 4*Keep me aware that while people are saying, "Peace and safety," destruction will come on them suddenly, as labor pains on a pregnant woman, and they will not escape, but I am not in darkness so that this day should surprise me like a thief. *5*Remind me often my King, that I am a son of the light and a son of the day and that I do not belong to the night or to the darkness. *6*Strengthen me Holy Spirit to not be like others who are asleep, but keep me alert and self-controlled. *7*Keep me aware of the fact that those who sleep, sleep at night, and those who get drunk, get drunk at night.

*8*Since I belong to the day my Father, I ask that you encourage me to be self-controlled. Remind me to put on faith and love as a breastplate, as well as the hope of salvation as a helmet. *9*Praise be to you O' God because you did not appoint me to suffer wrath, but rather to receive salvation through my Lord Jesus Christ. *10* Thank you Jesus for dying for me so that, whether I am awake or asleep, I may live together with you. *11*Therefore let me encourage others and build them up with that truth.

*12*Just now Lord, I ask you to keep me mindful to respect those who work hard among us, who are over us in the faith and who admonish us. *13*Help me I pray, to hold them in the highest regard in love because of their work and to live in peace with others. *14*Urge me to warn those who are idle, encourage the timid, help the weak and be patient with everyone. *15*Let me make sure that I never pay back wrong for wrong, but always try to be kind to others in the faith and to everyone else. *16, 17 & 18*I ask my King, that you help me to be joyful always, to pray continually and to give thanks in all circumstances, for this is your will for me in Christ Jesus. *19, 20, 21 & 22*Guide me Father God, to never put out the Spirit's fire; nor treat prophecies with contempt, but rather test everything and hold on to the good, as well as avoiding every kind of evil.

*23*May you O' God of peace, sanctify me through and through. I pray that my whole spirit, soul and body be kept blameless at the coming of my Lord Jesus Christ. *24*Thank you Lord for being faithful and for the faith to know that you will do it.

REFLECTIONS

The Book of 2nd Thessalonians

1 *²*Thank you Father God and you my Lord Jesus, for the grace and peace that I receive from you. *³*I pray that my faith would grow more and more, and my love for others would increase. *⁴*Strengthen me therefore in my perseverance and faith, as well as in all the persecutions and trials I am enduring or will face. *⁵* Help me to realize that the evidence of your judgment is always right and as a result I will be counted worthy of your kingdom O' God.

*⁶*Praise be to you Mighty God, for you are just and you will pay back trouble to those who trouble me. *⁷* Keep me aware Jesus, that this will happen when you are revealed from heaven in blazing fire with your powerful angels. *⁸*Also keep me attentive to the fact that you will punish those who do not know you or fail to obey your gospel. *⁹ & ¹⁰*They will be punished with everlasting destruction and shut out from your presence. How tragic my King, that they will also be excluded from the majesty of your power on the day you come to be glorified in your holy people and to be marveled at among all those who have believed; including me, because I believed your testimony.

*¹¹*With this in mind, I constantly pray that you, Heavenly Father; would count me worthy of your calling and that by your power fulfill every good purpose of mine and every act prompted by my faith. *¹²*I pray this so that the name of the Lord Jesus may be glorified in me according to your grace as my God.

2 *¹ & ²*Concerning your coming Lord Jesus and our being gathered to you, I ask that you never let me become easily unsettled or alarmed by some prophecy or statement that would say that day has already come. *³*I pray that I will never be deceived in any way and remain aware that your return will not come until the rebellion occurs and the man of lawlessness who is doomed to destruction is revealed. *⁴*Keep me aware that he will oppose and exalt himself over everything that is called God or is worshiped, so that he sets himself up in your temple, proclaiming himself to be God. *⁵ & ⁶*Help me to always remember that I was told these things and that I know what is holding him back, so that he may be revealed at the proper time.

*⁷*Let me bear in mind Master, that the secret power of lawlessness is already at work; but the one who now holds it back will continue to do so till he is taken out of the way. *⁸* After that, the lawless one will be revealed; whom you Lord Jesus will overthrow with the breath of your mouth and destroy by the splendor of your coming. *⁹ & ¹⁰*Keep me vigilant Jesus, concerning the coming of the lawless one. He will in accordance with the work of Satan; display all kinds of counterfeit miracles, signs, wonders and every sort of evil that deceives those who are perishing. You have taught me that they perish because they refused to love the truth and so be saved. *¹¹ & ¹²*For this reason Mighty God, you will send them a powerful delusion so that they will believe the lie and that all will be condemned who have not believed the truth, but have delighted in wickedness.

*¹³*I want to always thank you O' God, because from the beginning you chose me to be saved through the sanctifying work of the Spirit and through belief in the truth. *¹⁴*You called me to this gospel so that I might share in the glory of my Lord Jesus Christ. *¹⁵*Consequently, teach me to stand firm and hold to the teachings that were passed on to me. *¹⁶ & ¹⁷* May you my Lord Jesus and you God my Father, who loved me and by your grace gave me eternal encouragement and good hope; encourage my heart and strengthen me in every good deed and word.

3*¹*I pray that your message Lord may spread rapidly and be honored, just as it was with me. *²*I also pray that I may be delivered from wicked and evil men, since not everyone has faith. *³*Praise be that you my God because you are faithful; you will strengthen me and protect me from the evil one. *⁴*I have this confidence in you Lord; that you will sustain me in doing and continuing to do the things you command. *⁵*May you direct my heart in your love O' God and also in Christ's perseverance.

⁶It is your command Lord Jesus Christ, to keep away from every brother who is idle or does not live according to the teaching you have given. ⁷ & ⁸For that reason, I ought to follow your example. Keep me from being idle and to never let me eat anyone's food without paying for it. On the contrary, teach me to work night or day, laboring and toiling so that I will not be a burden to anyone. ⁹Remind me Lord I pray to do this, not because it is wrong to receive help; but in order to make myself a model for others to follow. ¹⁰Let me always take into account that the apostles gave this rule: "If a man will not work, he shall not eat."

¹¹I pray that I never be found idle, but instead busy; not just a busybody. ¹²Such people i.e. *"busybodies"* are commanded and urged by you Lord Jesus, to settle down and earn the bread they eat. ¹³As for me my King, encourage me to never tire of doing what is right. ¹⁴If anyone does not obey these instructions of yours Jesus, remind me to take special note of them and not associate with them in order that they may feel ashamed. ¹⁵Let me not regard them as an enemy, but warn them as a brother. ¹⁶May you the Lord of Peace; give me peace at all times and in every way and be with me always.

REFLECTIONS

The Book of 1st Timothy

1 [5]I pray Heavenly Father that you give me a pure heart, a good conscience and a sincere faith. [12]I thank you Christ Jesus, for giving me strength, for considering me faithful and for appointing me to your service. [13]I acknowledge that even though I was once a blasphemer, you had mercy on me. [14]Bless you Jesus, for pouring out your grace on me abundantly, along with giving me the faith and love that are in you.

[15]Help me remember that you came into the world to save sinners and I was just as guilty as the worst. [16]May I always bear in mind Savior that the very reason I was shown mercy was so that in me, you could display your unlimited patience as an example for those who would believe on you and receive eternal life. [17]Now to you my King the eternal, the immortal, the invisible, the only God; be honor and glory for ever and ever. [18]As your child, cause me to fight the good fight, [19]holding on to faith and a good conscience.

2 [1]I pray that you urge me to make requests, prayers, intercession and thanksgiving for everyone; [2]for leaders and all those in authority, that we may live peaceful and quiet lives in all godliness and holiness, because you, [3]God my Savior, [4]want all men to be saved and to come to a knowledge of the truth. [5]Thank you for being my mediator and [6]for giving yourself as a ransom for me. [8]Jesus, remind me to lift up holy hands in prayer, without anger or disputing.

3 [1]Since being an overseer is a noble task, [2]I pray that you help them to be above reproach, to be temperate, self-controlled, respectable, hospitable, able to teach and [3]dedicated to sobriety. Help them not to be violent, but gentle, not quarrelsome, nor a lover of money. [4]Heavenly Father, minister to them that they may manage their own family well and guide their children to obey them with proper respect. [6]Let them never become conceited and fall under the same judgment as the devil.

[7]Sustain their good reputation with outsiders, so that they will not fall into disgrace and into the devil's trap.

[8]Likewise I pray for deacons, that they too would remain men worthy of respect, sincere, dedicated to sobriety, and not pursuing dishonest gain. [9]I call upon you our Father, to encourage them to keep hold of the deep truths of the faith with a clear conscience. [11]I pray earnestly for their wives to be women worthy of respect, not malicious talkers but temperate and trustworthy in everything. [12]I ask that you consecrate the deacons to remain the husband of his one wife and guide him to manage his children and his household well.

4[1]Since the Spirit clearly says that in later times some will abandon the faith and follow deceiving spirits and things taught by demons; let me never [7]have anything to do with godless myths and old wives' tales, but rather train myself to be godly. [8]For physical training is of some value, but godliness has value for all things, holding promise for both the present life and the life to come. [9]Lord Jesus, bless me to set an example for other believers in speech, in life, in love, in faith and in purity.

[14]I pray that you remind me to never neglect your gift, which was given to me and to [15]be diligent in these matters; giving myself wholly to them, so that everyone may see my progress. [16]Father God, remind me to watch my life and doctrine closely and to persevere in them.

5[1]Heavenly Father, let me never rebuke an older man harshly, but exhort him as if he were my father. Remind me to treat younger men as brothers, [2]older women as mothers, and younger women as sisters, with absolute purity. [3]Let me and all the church, not forget to give proper recognition to those widows who are really in need. [8]Keep me mindful Father, that if anyone does not provide for his relatives, and especially for his immediate family, he has denied the faith and is worse than an unbeliever. [17]Since there are elders who direct the affairs of the church well, help me to give them double honor, especially those whose work is preaching and teaching. *²²*Lord Jesus protect me, so that I will not share in the sins of others and keep myself pure.

6/Jesus, give me the wisdom to realize that those who exercise authority over me are worthy of full respect, so that God's name and teaching may not be slandered. *²*If I have a believing master, help me not to show any less respect for them because they are brothers, but more. *⁵*Let me never be robbed of the truth by thinking that godliness is a means to financial gain, *⁶*but rather knowing that godliness with contentment is great gain. *⁷*For we brought nothing into the world, and we can take nothing out of it, *⁸*but if we have food and clothing, we will be content with that. *⁹*Father God, since people who want to get rich fall into temptation and a trap, keep me from the many foolish and harmful desires that plunge men into ruin and destruction. *¹⁰*Let me always remember that the love of money is the root of all kinds of evil and that some people, eager for money, have wandered from the faith and pierced themselves with many griefs. *¹¹*Help me O God, to flee from all this, and pursue righteousness, godliness, faith, love, endurance and gentleness.

*¹²*Strengthen me Father to fight the good fight of the faith and to take hold of the eternal life to which I was called. *¹³*In your sight O God, who gives life to everything, and to you Christ Jesus, who while testifying before Pontius Pilate made the good confession, let me always *¹⁴*keep your command without spot or blame until the appearing of my Lord Jesus Christ, *¹⁵*which you O God will bring about in your own time. You are the blessed and only Ruler, the King of kings and Lord of lords, *¹⁶*who is immortal and who lives in unapproachable light, whom no one has seen or can see. To you be honor and might forever.

*¹⁷*Master, let those who are rich in this present world not be arrogant, nor to put their hope in wealth, which is so uncertain, but encourage them to put their hope in you O God, who richly provides us with everything for our enjoyment.

*¹⁸*Let them do good things, be rich in good deeds, and be generous, as well as be willing to share. *¹⁹*In this way they will lay up treasure for

with him. If we disown him, he will also disown us; if we are faithless, he will remain faithful, for he cannot disown himself".

[14]My Father, keep reminding me that quarreling over words is of no value and only ruins those who listen. [15]Encourage me to do my best to present myself to you as one approved, a workman who does not need to be ashamed and who correctly handles the word of truth. [16,18]Help me avoid godless chatter, because if I indulge in it I will become more and more ungodly and wander away from the truth. [19]May I always bear in mind that your solid foundation stands firm, sealed with this inscription: "The Lord knows those who are his," and, "Everyone who confesses the name of the Lord must turn away from wickedness."

[20-21]Master, I realize that in a large house there are articles not only of gold and silver, but also of wood and clay. I pray that you help me recognize that some are for noble purposes and some for ignoble, and if I cleanse myself from the latter, I will be an instrument for noble purposes, made holy and useful to you, as well as being prepared to do any good work. [22]I also pray that you give me the courage and wisdom to flee evil desires and pursue righteousness, faith, love and peace. [23]Keep me from having anything to do with foolish and stupid arguments, because I know they produce quarrels. [24]I call upon you to enlighten me to the truth that your servants must not quarrel; instead, I must not only be kind to everyone, but also able to teach and never become resentful.

[25-26]Teach me to gently instruct those who oppose me, in the hope that you Mighty God, will grant them repentance. This will lead them to the knowledge of the truth, so that they will come to their senses and escape from the trap of the devil, who has taken them captive to do his will.

3[1]Heavenly Father, keep me ever conscious that there will be terrible times in the last days. [2]People will be lovers of themselves and lovers of money; they will be boastful, proud, abusive and disobedient to their parents, still more will be ungrateful and unholy. [3]They will be without love, unforgiving and slanderous, they will have no self-control, nor will they be lovers of the good; they will be brutal, [4]Also in the last days, people will be treacherous, rash and conceited; they will be lovers of pleasure rather than lovers of you, Mighty God. *⁵*They will have a form of godliness, but deny its power and I should have nothing to do with them. *⁶*They will be the kind who worm their way into homes and gain control over weak-willed people, who are loaded down with sins and are swayed by all kinds of evil desires. *⁷*They will be always learning, but never able to acknowledge the truth. *⁸⁻⁹*Help me also I pray, to realize that in the last days people with depraved minds will oppose the truth and who as far as the faith is concerned, should be rejected; but they will not get very far because their folly will be clear to everyone.

*¹⁰⁻¹¹*Thank you Father, for you have shown me all about the apostle's teachings; their way of life, their purpose, faith and patience, their love, endurance and persecutions, as well as their sufferings and what kinds of things happened to them along with how they endured their persecutions. Yet Lord, in your way, you rescued them from it all. *¹²*I ask that you strengthen me because; everyone who wants to live a godly life in Christ Jesus will be persecuted.

*¹³⁻¹⁵*Encourage me I pray, that even though evil men and impostors will go from bad to worse, deceiving and being deceived, I should continue in what I have learned and have become convinced of, because the Holy Scriptures are able to make me wise for salvation through faith in you Lord Jesus. *¹⁶⁻¹⁷*I pray to always keep foremost in my mind and in my heart that all Scripture is God-breathed and is useful for teaching, for rebuking and correcting, as well as training in righteousness, so that I may be thoroughly equipped for every good work.

4*¹*I call upon you, Lord Jesus, in view of your appearing and your kingdom, as well as you Heavenly Father, as the one who will judge the living and the dead, that you give me the presence of mind to fulfill the charge you have given. *²*Encourage me to preach the Word; to be prepared in season and out of season; to correct, rebuke and encourage with great patience and careful instruction. *³*I pray that you illuminate for me that the time will come when people will not put up with sound doctrine. Instead, to suit their own desires, they will gather around themselves a great number of teachers to say what their itching ears want to hear. ⁴I ask that you help me to understand that they will turn their ears away from the truth and turn aside to myths. ⁵Therefore Master, help me to keep my head in all situations and to endure hardship. Empower me to do the work of an evangelist and to discharge all the duties of my ministry.

⁶Prepare me my King, to be ever ready for the time of my departure, even if I am poured out like a drink offering. ⁷My Savior, I call upon your strength to fight the good fight, to finish the race and to keep the faith. ⁸Keep me ever aware that there is in store for me a crown of righteousness, which you, the righteous Judge, will award to me on that day; and not only to me, but also to all who have longed for your appearing. ¹⁸Thank you Lord for rescuing me from every evil attack and for bringing me safely to your heavenly kingdom. To you and you alone, be the glory for ever and ever.

REFLECTIONS

_____

_____

_____

_____

_____

_____

_____

_____

_____

_____

_____

_____

The Book of Titus

1 *1*My Heavenly Father, as your servant, I thank you for the faith and the knowledge of the truth that leads me to godliness. *2*I know that you cannot lie, so my faith and knowledge rests on the hope of eternal life, which you promised before the beginning of time. *3*Thank you, that at your appointed season, you brought your word to light through the preaching that was by your command, my Savior.

*6*I pray for our elders that they would be blameless and remain the husband of but one wife. I pray for their children to be believers and that they would not be open to the charge of being wild and disobedient. *7*Since an overseer is entrusted with your work Heavenly Father; I pray that they would be blameless, not overbearing, not quick-tempered, or given to drunkenness, not violent, nor pursuing dishonest gain. *8*I pray for our elders that they would be hospitable, lovers of what is good, self-controlled, upright, holy and disciplined. *9*I call upon you Mighty God, to encourage them to hold firmly to the trustworthy message as it has been taught, so that they can encourage others by sound doctrine and refute those who oppose it.

*15*Lord Jesus, let me as well as the elders never forget that to the pure, all things are pure, but to those who are corrupted and do not believe, nothing is pure. In fact, to the impure both their minds and consciences are corrupted. *16*They claim to know you, but by their actions they deny you. They are detestable, disobedient and unfit for doing anything good.

2 *1*Heavenly Father, forever guide me to teach what is in accord with sound doctrine.

*2*I pray that older men be temperate, worthy of respect, self-controlled, sound in faith, in love and in endurance. *3*Likewise I pray that, the older women be reverent in the way they live, not to be slanderers or addicted to much wine and to teach what is good. *4*Then they can train the younger women to love their husbands and children, *5*to be self-controlled and pure, to be busy at home, to be kind, and to be subject to their husbands, so that no one will malign your word O God. ⁶Similarly, I pray that you encourage the young men to be self-controlled.

⁷Lord Jesus, remind me in everything to set an example by doing what is good. In my teaching, bless me to show integrity, seriousness ⁸and soundness of speech that cannot be condemned, so that those who oppose you may be ashamed because they have nothing bad to say about us.

⁹Teach me Lord to be subject to my "boss" or "supervisor", to try to please them and not to talk back to them. ¹⁰Let me never steal from them, but show that I can be fully trusted, so that in every way I will make the teaching about you attractive. ¹¹For your grace, O God, brought salvation to me and all men. ¹²⁻¹³Bless you, because that grace teaches me to say "No" to ungodliness and worldly passions, as well as instructing me to live a self-controlled, upright and godly life in this present age, while I wait for the blessed hope; which is your glorious appearing.

¹⁴Thank you Jesus for giving yourself for me and redeeming me from all wickedness; thereby purifying me and making me part of a people that are your very own, eager to do what is good.

3¹Remind me Father, to be subject to rulers and authorities, to be obedient and to be ready to do whatever is good. ²Also, remind me to slander no one, to be peaceable, to be considerate and to show true humility toward all men. ³At one time I too was foolish, disobedient, deceived and enslaved by all kinds of passions and pleasures. I lived in malice and envy, being hated and hating others, ⁴but Savior, when your kindness and love appeared, ⁵you saved me, not because of righteous things I had done, but because of your mercy. You saved me through the washing of rebirth and renewal by the Holy Spirit, ⁶whom you poured out on me generously through Jesus Christ my Savior. ⁷Thank you Jesus, that having been justified by grace, I may now become an heir having the hope of eternal life.

⁸Keep me mindful Father of this trustworthy saying and stress these things to me, that since I have trusted in you O God, I should be careful to devote myself to doing what is good. These things are excellent and profitable for everyone. ⁹Let me always be alert to avoid foolish controversies and genealogies and arguments and quarrels about the law, because these are unprofitable and useless. ¹⁰Keep me aware that a divisive person should be warned once, and then warned a second time, after that, I should have nothing to do with them. ¹¹You have assured us all that such a person is warped, sinful and self-condemned. ¹⁴Finally my Father, cause me to learn to devote myself to doing what is good, in order that I may provide for daily necessities and not live an unproductive life.

REFLECTIONS

The Book of Philemon

1^{3}Father God, I thank you for your grace and peace. $^{4-5}$I want to always thank you in my prayers, as I remember the faith of the saints and their love of you my Lord Jesus. ^{6}I pray Jesus, to be active in sharing my faith, so that I will have a full understanding of every good thing I have in you. ^{7}Your love has given me great joy and encouragement, because it refreshes my heart and the hearts of the saints.

REFLECTIONS

_____
_____
_____
_____
_____
_____
_____
_____
_____
_____
_____
_____
_____
_____
_____
_____

The Book of Hebrews

1 *1-2*Father, it is clear that in the past you spoke to your people through the prophets at many times and in various ways, but in these last days you have spoken to us by your Son Jesus, whom you appointed heir of all things, and through whom you made the universe. *3*I worship you Jesus, because you are the radiance of God's glory and the exact representation of his being, sustaining all things by your powerful word. I glorify you because after you provided purification for sins, you sat down at the right hand of the Majesty in heaven. *4*You became as much superior to the angels as the name you inherited is superior to theirs.

*10*I pray that you help me grasp the scope of your greatness Lord, how in the beginning, you laid the foundations of the earth, and how the heavens are the work of your hands. *11*They will perish, but you remain; they will all wear out like a garment. *12*You will roll them up like a robe; like a garment they will be changed, but you remain the same and your years will never end.

2 *1*My Father, I ask therefore that you encourage me to pay more careful attention to what I have heard, so that I do not drift away. *2-3*Keep me aware that if the message spoken by angels was binding, and every violation and disobedience received its just punishment; how shall I escape if I ignore such a great salvation? Jesus, help me to realize the extent of this salvation that was first announced by you and was confirmed to those who originally heard you. *4*Thank you Mighty God for you also testified to it by signs, wonders and various miracles, as well as gifts of the Holy Spirit that were distributed according to your will.

*9*I am grateful to you, Jesus, because even though you were made a little lower than the angels, you are now crowned with glory and honor because you suffered death, so that by the grace of God you might taste death for me and everyone else. *10*I marvel O' God, at how fitting it is that you, through whom and for whom everything exists; would bring many sons to glory by making the author of my salvation perfect through suffering. *[11]*How marvelous it is that you, the one who makes me holy and those who are made holy, are of the same family, so much so that you are not ashamed to call us brothers.

*[14-15]*Master, I am so indebted to you given the fact that I have flesh and blood; you too shared in my humanity, so that by your death you destroyed the devil's power of death and freed all of us who were held in slavery by the fear of death. *[16]*Bless you, Jesus; for the surety that it is not angels that you help, but rather Abraham's descendants, of which I am now one. *[17]*Help me to comprehend that the reason you had to be made like a brother in every way; was so that you could become a merciful and faithful high priest in service to God, as well as making atonement for my sins and the sins of all people. *[18]*I will honor you because you suffered when you were tempted and are able to help us who are being tempted.

3*[1]*Therefore Jesus, since I now share in the heavenly calling, I will fix my thoughts on you, the apostle and high priest whom I confess. *[2]*Savior, empower me to be as faithful as you were to the one who appointed you. *[12]*My prayer is that I never have a sinful unbelieving heart that turns away from you Master. *[13]*Instead, cause me to encourage others daily, as long as it is called "Today", so that my heart will not be hardened by sin's deceitfulness. *[14]*Help me to see that I have come to share in all that you are, if I hold firmly till the end the confidence I had at first.

4*[1]*Father, I pray that you cause me to be careful not to fall short of the promise to enter your rest. *[2]*Help me to grasp that I, like the children of Israel, have had the gospel preached to me, just as they did; but the message they heard was of no value to them, because those who heard did not combine it with faith. *[4]*Give me insight and inspiration from the words spoken about the seventh day: "And on the seventh day God rested from all his work."

⁹Thank you, Mighty God, that there remains a "Sabbath" rest for us, your people. ¹⁰Encourage me to enter your rest and rest from my own work; just as you did from yours. ¹¹Strengthen me I pray, to make every effort to enter that rest, so that I will not fall by following the example of others' disobedience. ¹²I also pray that you encourage me with the truth that your word is living and active. Let me fully grasp how it is sharper than any double-edged sword and how it penetrates even to dividing soul and spirit, joints and marrow. Keep me mindful that it judges the thoughts and attitudes of the heart. ¹³I tremble in awe that nothing in all creation is hidden from your sight. Everything is uncovered and laid bare before your eyes and I must give an account.

¹⁴ Jesus, Son of God, because you are my great high priest who has gone through the heavens, I will hold firmly to the faith I profess. ¹⁵I worship you for the reason that you are a high priest who is able to sympathize with my weaknesses, yet even though you were tempted in every way (just like I am), you were and are without sin. ¹⁶Bless you for the confidence to approach the throne of grace, so that I may receive mercy and find grace to help me in my time of need.

5⁵⁻⁶Jesus, I pray that you help me realize the significance of you not taking upon yourself the glory of becoming a high priest during your life here on earth and may I also recognize that it was God who said to you, "You are my Son; today I have become your Father" and in another place, "You are a priest forever, in the order of Melchizedek." ⁷Help me genuinely understand; that during your days on earth, you offered up prayers and petitions with loud cries and tears to the one who could save you from death and you were heard because of your reverent submission. ⁸⁻⁹I glorify you, Master, in view of the fact that even though you were a son; you learned obedience from what you suffered and once made perfect, you became the source of eternal salvation for all who obey you. ¹⁰Thereby, you were designated by God to be high priest in the order of Melchizedek.

¹¹Forgive me, for even though there is much to be said about this; it is still hard for me to understand because I am so slow to learn. ¹²I am

shamed that by this time I should be a teacher, but instead I am satisfied to have someone to teach me the most elementary truths of your word all over again. My prayer is that I would become mature, not needing only milk, but rather solid food. *13*Help me to realize that anyone who lives on milk is still an infant and is not acquainted with the teaching about righteousness. *14*Lord, cause me to be grown-up on solid food, so that by its constant use I can train myself to distinguish good from evil.

REFLECTIONS

6*⁴⁻⁶*I pray that you keep me vigilant to the reality that once I have been enlightened, tasted the heavenly gift, shared in your Holy Spirit and have tasted the goodness of your word, as well as the powers of the coming age; that it is impossible to be brought back to repentance if I fall away, because to my loss; I would be crucifying the Son of God all over again and subjecting him to public disgrace. *⁷⁻⁸*Let me not forget that land that drinks in the rain often falling on it and that produces a crop useful to those for whom it is farmed receives your blessing, but land that produces thorns and thistles is worthless and is in danger of being cursed. In the end it will be burned.

*⁹*I thank you that in my case you have given me confidence of better things, that is to say; things that accompany salvation. *¹⁰*Father, you are worthy of my praise, because you are not unjust, you will not forget my work and the love I have shown as I help your people. *¹¹*I implore you for strength to show due diligence to the very end, in order to make my hope sure. *¹²*I want to never become lazy; instead cause me to imitate those who through faith and patience inherited what has been promised.

10*¹⁹*Jesus, I worship you because you have given me the confidence to enter the Most Holy Place by your blood! *²⁰*Bless you for the new and living way that was opened for me through the curtain, that is, your body. *²¹⁻²²*Since I have a great high priest over your house, Father God, cause me to draw near to you with a sincere heart in full assurance of faith, having my heart sprinkled to cleanse me from a guilty conscience and having my body washed with pure water. *²³*Because you are faithful, I pray that you strengthen me to hold unswervingly to the hope I profess. *²⁴*Also, cause me to consider how I may spur others on toward love and good deeds. *²⁵*Master, let me not give up meeting with believers, as some are in the habit of doing, but let me encourage others; and all the more as I see the Day approaching.

*²⁶⁻²⁷*My King, let me fearfully remember that if I deliberately keep on sinning after I have received the knowledge of the truth; no sacrifice for sins is left, but only a dreadful expectation of judgment and of raging fire that will consume your enemies.

*28*Let me also take into account that anyone who rejected the law of Moses died without mercy on the testimony of two or three witnesses. *29*How much more severely would I deserve to be punished if I trample the Son of God under foot and treat as an unholy thing the blood of the covenant that sanctified him, not to mention insulting the Spirit of grace. *30-31*Keep me aware that you will judge your people and that it can be a dreadful thing to fall into the hands of the living God.

*32*Strengthen me I pray, to always remember that I have received the light in order to stand my ground in the face of suffering or any great contest. *33*Prepare me in case I am publicly exposed to insult or persecution and give me the resolve to stand side by side with others who are so treated. *34*Let me sympathize with those in prison and joyfully accept the confiscation of my property, because I know that I will have better and longer lasting possessions. *35*I ask that you give me the resolve to never throw away my confidence because it will be richly rewarded. *36*Father, help me to persevere so that when I have done your will, I will receive what you have promised. *37*Jesus, allow me the spiritual insight to see that in just a very little while, you will come and will not delay. *38*I know that the righteous will live by faith and if I shrink back, you will not be pleased with me. *39*Keep me from ever shrinking back and being destroyed, but rather empower me to believe and be saved.

11 *1*My prayer is to live in the reality that faith is; being sure of what I hope for and certain of what I do not see. *2*Let me truly understand that this is what the ancients were commended for. *3*Father, it is by faith that I understand that the universe was formed at your command, so that what is seen was not made out of what was visible. *6*Let me never forget that without faith, it is impossible to please you, because when I come to you, I must believe that you exist and that you reward those who earnestly seek you.

12/Father God, since I am surrounded by such a great cloud of witnesses, encourage me to throw off everything that hinders and the sin that so easily entangles, so that I may run with perseverance the race marked out for me. *²*Jesus, cause me to fix my eyes on you, the author and developer of my faith. I am forever in your debt because; you endured the cross and scorned its shame, for the joy of sitting down at the right hand of God. *³*Since you are the one who endured such opposition from sinful men, make my meditations be about you, so that I will not grow weary and lose heart.

*⁴⁻⁶*I realize that in my struggle against sin, I have not yet resisted to the point of shedding my blood and I sometimes forget your words of encouragement when you address me as a son. May I never make light of your discipline, and never lose heart when you rebuke me. Open my understanding to the truth that you discipline those you love and you punish everyone you accept as a son. *⁷*Teach me I pray, to endure hardship as discipline, because you are treating me as a son and what son is not disciplined by his father?

*⁸*Train my way of thinking to realize that if I am not disciplined (and everyone undergoes discipline), then I am an illegitimate child and not a true son.

*¹⁰*Father God, I give thanks that you discipline me for my good, so that I may share in your holiness. *¹¹*I know that no discipline seems pleasant at the time and it is painful. Help me realize that later on, however, it produces a harvest of righteousness and peace for those who have been trained by it. *¹²*Therefore, encourage me to strengthen my feeble arms and weak knees. *¹³*I pray that you cause me to make level paths for my feet, so that I won't be lame or disabled, but rather healed.

*¹⁴*Help me make every effort to live in peace with all men and to be holy; because without holiness no one will see you, Lord. *¹⁵*Continue to guide me so that I will not fail to see your grace and a bitter root grow up that will cause trouble and defile me. *¹⁶*Keep me from sexual immorality, or godlessness like Esau, who for a single meal sold his inheritance rights as the oldest son.

13¹Keep aware, Father, that I should continue loving my fellow Christians as brothers. ²Do not let me forget to entertain strangers, for by so doing some people have entertained angels without knowing it. ³Cause me to remember those in prison as if I was their fellow prisoner, and those who are mistreated, as if I myself was suffering. ⁴Father, keep in my heart the truth that marriage should be honored by all and the marriage bed kept pure, for you will judge the adulterer and all the sexually immoral. ⁵Keep my life free from the love of money and teach me to be content with what I have, because you have said, "Never will I leave you; never will I forsake you." ⁶Let me be the one who says with confidence, "The Lord is my helper; I will not be afraid. What can man do to me?"

⁷I pray that you remind me often of Christian leaders, who spoke the word of God to me or others. Cause me to consider the outcome of their way of life and imitate their faith. ⁸I praise you Jesus, because you are the same yesterday and today and forever. ⁹Do not let me be carried away by any kind of strange teachings. Help me to see how good it is for my heart to be strengthened by grace. ¹⁵Through you Jesus, I pray to continually offer to God a sacrifice of praise, which is the fruit of lips that confess his name. ¹⁶Lord, let me not forget to do good and to share with others; for with such sacrifices you are pleased.

¹⁷Master, promote in me obedience to my leaders and submission to their authority. Teach me to take into account that they keep watch over us as men who must give an account. Help me to obey them, so that their work will be a joy, not a burden; for that would be of no advantage to me. ²⁰May I always remember that you are the God of peace, who through the blood of the eternal covenant brought back from the dead my Lord Jesus, who is the great Shepherd of the sheep. ²¹I pray that you equip me with everything good for doing your will, and may you work in me what is pleasing to you, through Jesus Christ, to whom be glory for ever and ever.

REFLECTIONS

_____

_____

_____

_____

_____

_____

_____

_____

_____

_____

_____

_____

_____

_____

_____

_____

_____

_____

_____

_____

_____

_____

_____

_____

_____

_____

_____

_____

_____

_____

_____

_____

The Book of James

1$^{2 \& 3}$My Heavenly Father, teach me how to consider it pure joy whenever I face trials of many kinds, because the testing of my faith develops perseverance. ^{4}May I always let perseverance finish its work so that I may be mature and complete, not lacking anything.

^{5}Help me to realize that anytime I lack wisdom, I should ask you because you give it generously to all without finding fault. ^{6}However, when I ask of you my King; teach me that I must believe and not doubt, because if I doubt I will become like a wave of the sea, blown and tossed by the wind.

$^{7 \& 8}$Let me comprehend that if I am like that, I should not think that I will receive anything from you Lord; because I would be double-minded and unstable in all that I do.

^{12}Let me always bear in mind that if I persevere under trial and when I stand the test; I will receive the crown of life that you have promised to those who love you. ^{13}Lord, when I am tempted let me never say that you are tempting me, because you cannot be tempted by evil, nor do you tempt anyone. ^{14}Help me realize that when I am tempted, it is by my own evil desire that I am dragged away and enticed. ^{15}Then, after desire has conceived, it gives birth to sin; and sin, when it is full-grown, gives birth to death.

$^{16 \& 17}$Don't let me be deceived, let me learn from my heart that every good and perfect gift is from above, coming down from you; the Father of the heavenly lights, who does not change like shifting shadows. ^{18}You chose to give me birth through the word of truth, that I might be a kind of first fruit of all you created.

$^{19 \& 20}$My Father, let me grasp that I should be quick to listen, slow to speak and slow to become angry, for my anger does not bring about the righteous life that you desire. ^{21}Therefore, help me to get rid of all moral filth and the evil that is so prevalent and humbly accept the word planted in me, which can save me.

*22*Teach me to not merely listen to the word, and so deceive myself; but do what it says! *23 & 24*Let me realize if I listen to the word, but do not do what it says; it is like a man who looks at his face in a mirror and after looking at himself, goes away and immediately forgets what he looks like. *25*Help me to understand that if I look intently into the perfect law that gives freedom, and continues to do this, not forgetting what I have heard, but doing it, I will be blessed in whatever I do.

*26*If I am to consider myself religious and yet do not keep a tight rein on my tongue; let it be clear in my heart that I am deceiving myself and my "religion" is worthless. *27*Remind me often that religion that you accept as pure and faultless is this: to look after orphans and widows in their distress and to keep myself from being polluted by the world.

2*1*My Lord Jesus, as a believer in you, do not let me show favoritism. *2-4*If a man comes into a meeting wearing a gold ring and fine clothes, and a poor man in shabby clothes also comes in and I show special attention to the man wearing fine clothes by saying, "Here's a good seat for you," but say to the poor man, "You stand there" or "Sit at a less desirable seat," have I not discriminated and become a judge with evil thoughts? *5*Let me always take into account that you, Mighty God, have chosen those who are poor in the eyes of the world to be rich in faith and to inherit the kingdom you promised to those who love you.

*8 & 9*Have me always consider that if I really keep the royal law found in Scripture, "Love my neighbor as myself," I am doing right, but if I show favoritism, I sin and am convicted by the law as a lawbreaker. *10*Let me not forget that whoever keeps the whole law and yet stumbles at just one point is guilty of breaking all of it. *12 & 13*Guide me I pray, to speak and act as one who is going to be judged by the law that gives freedom; because judgment without mercy will be shown to me if I have not been merciful. Help me appreciate that mercy triumphs over judgment! *14*Let me realize that if I claim to have faith, but have no deeds, that such a faith cannot save me.

*15 & 16*Let me bear in mind that if a brother or sister is without clothes or daily food and I say to them, "Go, I wish you well; keep warm and well fed," but do nothing about their physical needs, what good is it? *17*In the same way, help me to recognize that faith by itself, if it is not accompanied by action, is dead. *18*Even though some may say, "You have faith; I have deeds." Show them through me that I display my faith by what I do. *19*I believe that you are the one and only God and even though that is good, may I always bear in mind that even the demons believe that and shudder. *20*Keep me from being deceived and foolish by realizing that faith without deeds is useless. *26*Illuminate for me the truth that as the body without the spirit is dead, so faith without deeds is dead.

3*1*Heavenly Father, let it be clear in my heart that those who teach will be judged more strictly. *2*I know that I stumble in many ways and if I am never at fault in what I say, I would be a perfect man, able to keep my body in check. *5*May I always be mindful that my tongue is a small part of my body, but it makes great boasts. Likewise, let me consider that a great forest is set on fire by a small spark. *6*Help me to recognize, that the tongue also is a fire, a world of evil among the parts of the body. It corrupts the whole person, sets the whole course of a person's life on fire, and is itself set on fire by hell.

*7 & 8*Master, all kinds of animals, birds, reptiles and creatures of the sea are being tamed and have been tamed by man, but no man can tame the tongue. It is a restless evil, full of deadly poison. *9*I confess that with my tongue I praise you Lord and Father, and yet with it I also curse men, who have been made in your likeness. *10*Out of my mouth come praise and cursing, Master this should not be! *11* Can both fresh water and salt water flow from the same spring? *12*My Father, let me not forget that a fig tree cannot bear olives, or a grapevine bear figs? Consequently neither can a salt spring produce fresh water.

¹³My King, if I am to be wise and understanding, let me show it by my good life and by deeds done in the humility that come from wisdom. ¹⁴But if I should ever harbor bitter envy and selfish ambition in my heart, let me not boast about it or deny the truth. ¹⁵Instead may I quickly realize such "false wisdom" does not come down from heaven but is earthly, unspiritual, of the devil.

¹⁶Help me recognize that if I have envy and selfish ambition, that there I will find disorder and every evil practice. ¹⁷May I always bear in mind that the wisdom that comes from heaven is first of all pure; then peace-loving, considerate, submissive, full of mercy and good fruit, impartial and sincere. ¹⁸Help me I pray to become conscious that peacemakers who sow in peace raise a harvest of righteousness.

4¹Master, may I always take into account what causes fights and quarrels; which is the desires that battle within me. ²I may want something, but don't get it. I may even kill and covet, but I cannot have what I want and I do not have, because I do not ask of you O' God. ³When I ask, I do not receive, because I ask with wrong motives so that I may spend what I get on my pleasures.

⁴ Forgive me I pray for being adulterous and not considering that friendship with the world is hatred toward you. Keep me mindful that anyone who chooses to be a friend of the world becomes an enemy of you. ⁵Let me take into account that the Scriptures do not say without reason that the spirit you caused to live in me envies intensely. ⁶Thank you for giving me more grace! Which is why Scripture says: "God opposes the proud, but gives grace to the humble."

⁷May I fully realize that if I submit myself to you Mighty God and resist the devil, that he will flee from me. ⁸ Help me to become conscious that if I come near to you that you will come near to me. Let me wash my hands, purify my heart and not be double-minded. ⁹Move me Holy Spirit to grieve, mourn and wail. Change my laughter to mourning and my joy to gloom. ¹⁰ Teach me to humble myself before you so that you will lift me up.

*11*My Father, do not let me ever slander another, for if I speak against my brother or judge him; I speak against the law and judge it. May I ever bear in mind that when I judge the law, I am not keeping it, but sitting in judgment on it. *12*You O' God are the one and only Lawgiver and Judge, the one who is able to save and destroy; therefore who am I to judge my neighbor?

*13*Now may I be careful not to say, "Today or tomorrow I will go to this or that city, spend a year there, carry on business and make money." *14*Help me to always consider that I do not even know what will happen tomorrow. What is my life? I am merely a mist that appears for a little while and then vanishes. *15*Instead, teach me to say, "If it is your will, I will live and do this or that." *16*As it is, I could boast or brag and all such boasting is evil. *17*If then, I know the good I ought to do and do not do it, I commit a sin.

5*7*Teach me I pray to be patient, until you come again. Let me realize how the farmer waits for the land to yield its valuable crop and how patient he is for the autumn and spring rains. *8*Train me also to be patient and stand firm, because your coming is near. *9*Don't allow me to grumble against others, for I also will be judged and you as the Judge are standing at the door! *10*Illuminate for me the example of patience the prophets who spoke in your name Lord in the face of suffering. *11*As you have instructed, I should consider blessed those who have persevered. You have taught me of Job's perseverance and what you finally brought about; bless you Lord for you are full of compassion and mercy. *12*Above all, my Father, strengthen me to not swear--not by heaven, nor by earth, or by anything else. May my "Yes" always be yes, and my "No," always be no, else wise I will be condemned.

*13*Encourage me to always keep in mind that if I am in trouble, I should pray. If I am happy, I should sing songs of praise. *14&15*If I am sick, I should call the elders of the church to pray over me and anoint me with oil in your name, Lord, and the prayer offered in faith will make me well and you will raise me up. If I have sinned, I will be forgiven. *16*Therefore, teach me to confess my sins to others and pray for others so that I may be healed. Help me to remember that the prayer of a righteous man is powerful and effective.

[17 & 18]Lord, may I realize that Elijah was a man just like me. He prayed earnestly that it would not rain, and it did not rain on the land for three and a half years, but when he prayed again the heavens gave rain, and the earth produced its crops. [19 & 20]My Father, if a Christian should wander from the truth and I am the one who brings him back, let me take into account that: "Whoever turns a sinner from the error of his way will save him from death and cover over a multitude of sins".

REFLECTIONS

_____
_____
_____
_____
_____
_____
_____
_____
_____
_____
_____
_____
_____
_____
_____

The Book of 1st Peter

1^{1} Thank you Jesus, for making me a disciple, one of whom you chose to be a stranger in the world. ^{2}Thank you God my Father for choosing me according to your foreknowledge, through the sanctifying work of the Spirit, the obedience to Jesus Christ and the sprinkling by his blood. May your grace and your peace be always mine in abundance!

^{3}Praise be to you O God, the Father of my Lord Jesus Christ! In your great mercy, you have given me a new birth into a living hope through the resurrection of Jesus Christ from the dead. ^{4}You have also given me an inheritance that is kept in heaven that can never perish, spoil or fade ^{5}Thank you, that through faith, I am shielded by your power O God, until the coming of the salvation that is ready to be revealed in the last time. ^{6}In this I greatly rejoice, though now for a little while I may have to suffer grief in all kinds of trials. ^{7}These have come so that my faith, which is of greater worth than gold which perishes, may be proved genuine. I pray that my faith may result in praise, glory and honor when Jesus Christ is revealed. ^{8}Father, even though I have not seen Jesus, I love him; and even though I do not see him now, I believe in him and am filled with an inexpressible and glorious joy, ^{9}for I am receiving the goal of my faith; the salvation of my soul.

^{13}It is my prayer therefore Mighty God, that you prepare my mind for action. I pray to be self-controlled and guided to set my hope fully on the grace to be given me when Jesus Christ is revealed. ^{14}I pray that you cause me to be an obedient child and not conform to the evil desires I had when I lived in ignorance. ^{15}Just as you who called me are holy; help me to be holy in all I do; ^{16}for you have written: "Be holy, because I am holy."

^{17}Since I call on you my Father; who judges each man's work impartially, teach me to live my life as a stranger here in reverent fear. ^{18}Let me never forget that it was not with perishable things such as silver or gold that I was redeemed from the empty way of life handed down to me, ^{19}but with the precious blood of Christ, a lamb without blemish or defect. ^{20}Remind me often Jesus, that you were chosen before the creation of the world, but are revealed in these last times for my sake. *21*Through you I believe in God, who raised you from the dead and glorified you, and so my faith and hope are in you Jesus. *22*Now that I have purified myself by obeying the truth so that I have sincere love for my brothers; let me love them deeply, from my heart. *23*For I have been born again, not of perishable seed, but of imperishable, through the living and enduring word of God. *24*For, "All men are like grass, and all their glory is like the flowers of the field; the grass withers and the flowers fall, *25* but your word O Lord stands forever." And this is the word that was preached to me.

2*1*Therefore my King, strengthen me to rid myself of all malice, deceit, hypocrisy, envy, and slander of every kind. *2*Like a newborn baby, cause me to crave pure spiritual milk, so that by it I may grow up in your salvation, *3*now that I have tasted that you my Lord, are good. *4*As I come to you, the living Stone, (rejected by men but precious and chosen by God) *5*I also, like a living stone, am being built into the spiritual house to be a holy priest, offering spiritual sacrifices acceptable to you O God through Jesus Christ.

*9*Thank you my Father for making me one of your chosen people, part of a royal priesthood, a holy nation and a people belonging to you O God, so that I may declare the praises of the one who called me out of darkness into your wonderful light. *10*Once I was not one of your people, but now I am; once I had not received mercy, but now I have received your mercy.

*11*Urge me Holy Spirit, as an alien and a stranger in the world, to abstain from sinful desires, which war against my soul. *12*Teach me to live such a good life among the pagans that, though they accuse me of doing wrong, they may see my good deeds and glorify you my Father on the day you visit us.

13 For your sake Lord, compel me to submit myself to every authority instituted among men: whether to the head of nations, as the supreme authority, *14*or to governors, who are sent by you to punish those who do wrong and to commend those who do right. *¹⁵*For it is your will O God that by doing good I should silence the ignorant talk of foolish men. *¹⁶*Let me live always as a free man, but never using my freedom as a cover-up for evil. Let me live as your servant mighty God! *¹⁷*Teach me proper respect to everyone: to love the brotherhood of believers, to fear you as my God and honor my country's leaders.

*¹⁸*Master, help me to submit to my "boss" with all respect, not only if they are good and considerate, but also if they are harsh. *¹⁹*I know it is commendable if a man bears up under the pain of unjust suffering because he is conscious of you O God. *²⁰*Let me never forget that it is not to my credit or commendable before you, if I am chastised for doing wrong and endure it. *²¹*To this I was called; because you Jesus suffered for me, leaving me an example, that I should follow in your steps. *²²*You committed no sin, and no deceit was found in your mouth. *²³*When they hurled their insults at you, you did not retaliate; when you suffered, you made no threats. Instead, you entrusted yourself to the God of Heaven who judges justly. *²⁴*You bore my sins in your body on the tree, so that I might die to sin and live for righteousness; by your wounds I have been healed. *²⁵*For I was like a sheep going astray, but now I have returned to you, the Shepherd and Overseer of my soul.

3*¹*Heavenly Father, I pray for women who are wives, that in the same way they would be submissive to their husbands, so that if their husbands do not believe your word, they may be won over without words by the behavior of their wives, *²*when they see the purity and reverence of their lives.

*³*Reveal to them that their beauty should not come from outward adornment, *⁴*instead, it should be that of their inner self, the unfading beauty of a gentle and quiet spirit, which is of great worth in your sight. *⁵*I pray that you remind them that this is the way the holy women of the past used to make themselves beautiful; they were submissive to their own husbands. *⁶*Help them Father to do what is right and to not give way to fear. *⁷*In the same way, I pray that husbands be considerate as they live with their wives, and treat them with respect as the weaker partner and as heirs with you of the gracious gift of life, so that nothing will hinder their prayers.

*⁸*Teach me, my Master, to live in harmony with others; to be sympathetic, to love as a brother and to be compassionate and humble. *⁹*I pray that you also teach me to never repay evil with evil or insult with insult, but with blessing; because to this I was called so that I may inherit a blessing. *¹⁰*For, "Whoever would love life and see good days must keep his tongue from evil and his lips from deceitful speech."

*¹¹*Therefore I must turn from evil and do good; I must seek peace and pursue it. *¹²*For your eyes O Lord, are on the righteous and your ears are attentive to my prayer. Let me never forget Lord that your face is against those who do evil, *¹⁴*but even if I should suffer for what is right, I will be blessed. Encourage me not to fear what unbelievers fear and not be frightened. *¹⁵*Teach me Christ Jesus; to set you apart as Lord in my heart and to always be prepared to give an answer to everyone who asks me to give the reason for the hope that I have. Help me to always do this with gentleness and respect, *¹⁶*keeping a clear conscience, so that those who speak maliciously against my good behavior in you Christ Jesus may be ashamed of their slander.

4Therefore Jesus, since you suffered in your body, teach me to arm myself with the same attitude, because if I suffer in my body, I am done with sin. *²*As a result, I will not live the rest of my earthly life for evil human desires, but rather for your will mighty God. *³*Let me never forget that I have spent enough time in the past doing what pagans choose to do.

*⁷*Heavenly Father, since the end of all things is near; I ask that you bless me to be clear-minded and self-controlled so that I can pray. *⁸*Above all, teach me to love others deeply, because love covers over a multitude of sins. *⁹*Remind me often Master, to offer hospitality to others without grumbling, *¹⁰*and to use whatever gifts I have received to serve others, faithfully administering your grace in its various forms. *¹¹*Whenever I speak; let me do it as one speaking your very words, O God. When I serve, let it be with the strength you provide, so that in all things, you the great God of heaven may be praised.

*12*Father God, bless me to never be surprised at any painful trial that I may suffer, as though something strange may be happening to me; *13*instead teach me to rejoice that I participate in the sufferings of Christ, so that I may be overjoyed when your glory is revealed.

*14*If I am insulted because of the name of Christ, I am blessed; for the Spirit of glory and you O God rests on me. *16* If I should ever suffer as a Christian, remind me to not be ashamed, but praise you that I bear your name. *17*For it is time for judgment to begin with the family of God; and if it begins with me, what will the outcome be for those who do not obey the gospel? *18*Also, "If it is hard for the righteous to be saved, what will become of the ungodly and the sinner?" *19*So then, as one who may have to suffer according to your will, show me how to commit myself to you my faithful Creator and help me to continue doing good.

5*1*I pray for the elders among us, *2*to be shepherds of your flock that are under their care. I pray that they would serve as overseers; not because they must, but because they are willing, as you O God want them to be. I ask that you help them to never be greedy for money, but eager to serve; *3*not lording it over those entrusted to them, but being examples to the flock, *4*so that when you as the Chief Shepherd appear, they will receive the crown of glory that will never fade away.

*5*Shape me Master in the same way to be submissive to those who are older. Direct me to clothe myself with humility toward others, because you oppose the proud, but give grace to the humble. *6*Help me to humble myself under your hand, mighty God, so that you may lift me up in due time. *7*I pray that you train me to cast all my anxiety on you because you care for me. *8*I ask that you strengthen me to be self-controlled and alert, because my enemy the devil prowls around like a roaring lion looking for someone to devour. *9*Consequently, encourage me to resist him, standing firm in the faith, because I know that my brothers throughout the world are undergoing the same kind of sufferings. *10*Thank you, the

God of all grace, who called me to your eternal glory in Christ, that after I have suffered a little while, will restore me and make me strong, firm and steadfast. *¹¹*To you be the power for ever and ever.

REFLECTIONS

_____

_____

_____

_____

_____

_____

_____

_____

_____

_____

_____

_____

_____

_____

_____

_____

_____

_____

The Book of 2ⁿᵈ Peter

1 ¹Thank you Heavenly Father that through your righteousness and my Savior Jesus Christ, I have received a precious faith. ²I am grateful for the grace and peace that is mine in abundance through the knowledge of your love. ³Your divine power has given me everything I need for life and godliness through my knowledge of you because you have called me by your own glory and goodness. ⁴Through these I have been given your very great and precious promises, so that through them I may participate in the divine nature and escape the corruption in the world caused by evil desires.

⁵For this very reason, I pray that you strengthen me to make every effort to add to my faith, goodness; and to goodness, knowledge; ⁶and to knowledge, self-control; and to self-control, perseverance; and to perseverance, godliness; ⁷and to godliness, brotherly kindness; and to brotherly kindness, love. ⁸Lord Jesus, let me not forget that if I possess these qualities in increasing measure, they will keep me from being ineffective and unproductive in my knowledge of you. ⁹ Help me to also realize that if I do not have them; I am nearsighted and blind, and have forgotten that I have been cleansed from my past sins.

¹⁰ & ¹¹Therefore my Savior, encourage me to be all the more eager to make my calling and election sure. For if I do these things, I will never fall and I will receive a rich welcome into your eternal kingdom. ¹²I beseech you my King, to always remind me of these things, even though I know them and am firmly established in the truth I now have. ¹³ & ¹⁴I know that it is right to refresh my memory as long as I live in the tent of this body, because I know that I will one day put it aside, as you have made clear to me. ¹⁵Help me, I pray, to make every effort to see that after my departure, others will always be able to remember these things.

¹⁶Keep me mindful Lord Jesus, that I did not follow a cleverly invented story when I was told about you, your power and your return, but I am a witness of your majesty. ¹⁷For you received honor and glory from God the Father when the voice came to you from the Majestic Glory, saying,

"This is my Son, whom I love; with him I am well pleased." *¹⁸*Let me not forget that this voice that came from heaven was heard by reliable witnesses when they were with you Jesus, on the sacred mountain. *¹⁹*Additionally, I have the word of the prophets made more certain, and I will do well to pay attention to it, as to a light shining in a dark place, until the day dawns and the morning star rises in my heart. *²⁰*Above all Father God, help me understand that no prophecy of Scripture came about by the prophet's own interpretation. *²¹*For prophecy never had its origin in the will of man, but men spoke from you O' God, as they were carried along by the Holy Spirit.

2 *¹*Master, keep me ever aware that there were also false prophets among the people at that time, just as there are and will be false teachers among us now. They will secretly introduce destructive heresies, even denying you, the sovereign Lord who bought them; bringing swift destruction on themselves.

² Help me I pray, to realize that many will follow their shameful ways and will bring the way of truth into disrepute. *³*Keep me mindful that in their greed these teachers will try to exploit people with stories they have made up. Their condemnation has long been hanging over them, and their destruction has not been sleeping.

*⁴*For if you Mighty God, did not spare angels when they sinned, but sent them to hell, putting them into gloomy dungeons to be held for judgment; *⁵*if you my King did not spare the ancient world when you brought the flood on its ungodly people, but protected Noah, a preacher of righteousness, and seven others; *⁶*if you the great Judge, condemned the cities of Sodom and Gomorrah by burning them to ashes, and made them an example of what is going to happen to the ungodly; *⁷*and if you Heavenly Father rescued Lot, a righteous man, who was distressed by the filthy lives of lawless men… *⁹*if this is so, then you O' Lord know how to rescue godly men from trials and to hold the unrighteous for the day of judgment, while continuing their punishment.

*10 & 11*Keep me constantly aware regarding your judgment my King, especially concerning those who follow the corrupt desire of the sinful nature and despise authority. *19*Let it always be foremost in my mind, that a man is a slave to whatever has mastered him. *20*Since I have escaped the corruption of the world by having you as my Lord and Savior, and if ever again I become overcome and entangled in it; then I will be worse off at the end than I was at the beginning. *21*It would have been better for me not to have known the way of righteousness, than to have known it and then to turn my back on the sacred command that was passed on to me.

3*/*Dear Father in Heaven, I pray that you stimulate me to wholesome thinking. *2*I want to recall often the words spoken in the past by the holy prophets and the commands given by my Lord and Savior. *3*Help me my King to understand that in the last days scoffers will come, ridiculing and following their own evil desires. *4*They will say, "Where is this return he promised? Ever since our fathers died, everything goes on as it has since the beginning of creation." *5*Keep me attentive to the fact that they deliberately forget, that long ago by your words O' God; the heavens existed and the earth was formed out of water and by water. *6*By these waters also the world of that time was deluged and destroyed. *7*By the same word the present heavens and earth are reserved for fire, being kept for the Day of Judgment and destruction of ungodly men.

*8*Master do not let me ever forget this one thing: With you, a day is like a thousand years, and a thousand years are like a day. *9*Let me always bear in my mind; that you Lord are not slow in keeping your promise, as some understand slowness. You are patient with us, not wanting anyone to perish, but rather wanting everyone to come to repentance. *10*Keep me mindful I pray, of the fact that the day of the Lord will come like a thief. The heavens will disappear with a roar; the elements will be destroyed by fire, and the earth and everything in it will be laid bare.

*11 & 12*Since everything will be destroyed in this way, what kind of person should I be? Therefore my King, strengthen me to live a holy and godly life, as I look forward to that day and speed its coming. That day will bring about the destruction of the heavens by fire, and the elements will melt in the heat. *¹³*But in keeping with your promise I am looking forward to a new heaven and a new earth, the home of righteousness.

*¹⁴*Since then I am looking forward to this; strengthen me to make every effort to be found spotless, blameless and at peace with you my King. *¹⁵*Help me I pray to bear in mind; that your patience Lord means salvation. *¹⁷*Let me always be on your guard Jesus, so that I may not be carried away by the error of lawless men and fall from my secure position. *¹⁸*Bless me to grow in the grace and knowledge of you my Savior, to whom belongs the glory both now and forever!

REFLECTIONS

_____
_____
_____
_____
_____
_____
_____
_____
_____
_____
_____
_____
_____
_____
_____
_____
_____
_____

The Book of 1st John

1 *1*Praise to you Jesus, for you are the Word of life that was from the beginning, from whom I have heard, who has actually been seen by the eyes of men and touched with their hands. *2*Your life appeared and was witnessed by men who have testified about it and now proclaimed to be the eternal life which was with the Father and confirmed to mankind. *3*May I also proclaim to others what I have seen and heard, so that they will have fellowship with you Father and with Jesus. *4*Let me keep in mind that this is what will make my joy complete.

*5*Thank you for the message I have heard and now declare: that you O' God are the light and in you there is no darkness at all. *6*Let me always bear in mind that if I claim to have fellowship with you, yet walk in the darkness; I am a liar and do not live by the truth. *7*Cause me I pray, to walk in the light as you are in the light, so that I will have fellowship with other Christians and your blood Jesus, will purify us from all sin. *8*Master, help me to always bear in mind that if I claim to be without sin, I deceive myself and the truth is not in me. *9*I am thankful that if I confess my sin, that you are faithful and just to forgive me of my sin and purify me from all unrighteousness. *10*If I claim that I have not sinned, I make you out to be a liar and your word has no place in my life.

2 *1*Heavenly Father I pray that I would not sin; but if I do sin, I am thankful that I have Jesus the Righteous One to speak to you in my defense. *2*Thank you Jesus for being the atoning sacrifice for my sins and not only for mine, but also for the sins of the whole world! *3*I realize that I have come to know you if I obey your commands. *4, 5 & 6*Help me take into account that if I say "I know him," but I do not do what you command, I am a liar and the truth is not in me; but if I obey your word Jesus, your love is truly made complete in me. This is how I will know I am in you Jesus: that if I claim to live in you, I must walk as you did.

*7*Master, help me realize that you are not giving me a new command, but an old one which has been since the beginning. This old command is the message I have heard. [8]Yet in many ways you are giving me a new understanding which is: the truth I see in Jesus, is because the darkness is passing and the true light is already shining. [9]Keep me aware Master, that if I claim to be in the light, but hate my brother; I am still in the darkness. [10 & 11]May I learn by heart that if I love my brother, I live in the light and there is nothing in me to make me stumble, but if I hate my brother, I am in the darkness and walk around in it; I do not know where I am going, because the darkness has blinded me.

[12]I thank you Jesus because my sins have been forgiven on account of your name. [13] Thank you for allowing me to know the one who is and was from the beginning. Thank you because you have made me able to overcome the evil one. Thank you for providing me access to know you Father. [15]Compel me I pray, not to love the world or anything in the world. Help me to realize that if I love the world: your love Father is not in me. [16]Keep me aware I pray, that everything in the world; my sinful cravings, the lust of my eyes and the boasting of what I have, or my abilities does not come from you Heavenly Father, but from the world. [17]May I never forget that the world and its desires pass away, but if I do your will, I will live forever.

[18]Master, I ask that you help me consider that this is the last hour and as I have heard that the antichrist is coming, may I also consider that even now many antichrists have already come. This is how I am to know that it is the last hour. [19]Let me grasp that these "antichrists" came out of the church, but they did not really belong to your church; for if they had belonged to your church, they would have remained there. Their going showed that none of them truly belonged to you. [20]Thank you my King for the anointing from the Holy One and for the truth.

[21]You have shown me the truth and I also know that no lie comes from the truth. [22]Who then is the liar? It is the man who denies that you Jesus are indeed the Christ. Such a man is the antichrist because he denies the Father and the Son. [23]May I always keep in mind that anyone who denies the Son also denies you Father and whoever acknowledges the Son has the Father also. [24 & 25]Encourage me I pray, to see to it that what

I have heard from the beginning remains in me; because if it does, I will remain in you Jesus, as well as remaining in you my Heavenly Father and this is what you promised me; eternal life.

²⁶I pray Father that you illuminate these things for me about those who would try to lead me astray. ²⁷I honor you because the anointing I received from you remains in me and I do not need anyone else to teach me. Remind me often that it is your anointing that teaches me about all things and as that anointing is real, not counterfeit; I am taught to remain in you. ²⁸Compel me I pray to continue in you Lord Jesus, so that when you appear, I may be confident and unashamed before you at your coming. ²⁹Since I know that you are righteous, may I take into account that everyone who does what is right has been born of you Lord.

3[/]How great is your love that you lavish on me Father, that I should be called your child! The reason the world does not know me is, that it does not know you. ²Give me an understanding that even though I am one of your children, what I will be has not yet been made known, but I know that when Jesus appears; I shall be like him, for I shall see him as he is. ³Lord, since I have this hope in me, cause me to purify myself, just as you are pure. ^{4 & 5}Let me keep in mind that everyone who sins; breaks the law. In fact, sin is lawlessness, but I also know that you Jesus appeared so that you would take away my sins and in you is no sin. ⁶Keep me conscious of the fact that: No one who lives in you keeps on sinning and that no one who continues to sin has either seen you or known you.

⁷I pray that I am never led astray and am always aware that he who does what is right is righteous, just as you are righteous. ⁸May I also bear in mind that he who does what is sinful is of the devil, because the devil has been sinning from the beginning. Lord Jesus, help me to fully grasp that the reason you appeared was to destroy the devil's work. ⁹Keep me in remembrance Mighty God, that since I have been born of you, I will not continue to sin because your seed remains in me; I cannot go on sinning, because I have been born of you. ¹⁰Help me to truly understand that this is how to know who your children are and who the children of the devil are: Anyone who does not do what is right is not one of your

children; nor is anyone who does not love his brother. *11*Let me recognize that the message I have heard from the beginning is; that I should have love for others.

*12*Compel me Jesus, to never be like Cain who belonged to the evil one and murdered his brother because his own actions were evil and his brother's were righteous. *13*Father, teach me to not be surprised if the world hates me. *14* Thank you for showing me that I have passed from death to life because I love my brothers. Keep me mindful that if I do not love others I remain in death. *15*Also let me bear in mind that if I hate my brother I am a murderer and that no murderer has eternal life in him.

*16*Jesus, help me to recognize how to know what love is, which is: That you the Lamb of God, laid down your life for me and I ought to lay down my life for my brothers. *17*Keep me conscious that if I have material possessions and see my brother in need, but have no pity on him; how can the love of God be in me?

*18*My Father, do not let me love with just words or tongue, but with actions and in truth. *19 & 20*Let me discover, that this is how I will know that I belong to the truth and how I set my heart at rest in your presence whenever my heart condemns me, because you O' God are greater than my heart and you know everything.

*21 & 22*I am thankful Master that if my heart does not condemn me, I have confidence before you and receive from you anything I ask, because I obey your commands and because I do what pleases you. *23*Keep me ever mindful that this is your command: To believe in the name of your Son, Jesus Christ, and to love others as you have instructed me. *24*I ask that you train me to obey your commands, so I may live in you and you may live in me. This is how I will know that you live in me: I will know it by the Spirit you gave me.

4*1*Mighty God, I pray that I would not believe every spirit, but test the spirits to see whether they are from you, because many false prophets have gone out into the world. *2 & 3*Help me to recognize your Holy Spirit, which is by distinguishing that: Every spirit that acknowledges that

Jesus Christ has come in the flesh is from you, but every spirit that does not acknowledge Jesus is not from you. Keep me conscious that this is the spirit of the antichrist; which I have heard is coming and even now is already in the world.

*4*May I always bear in mind Heavenly Father, that as one of your dear children, I am from you and I can overcome the world, because your greatness in me is superior to the one who is in the world. *5*Those who are from the world speak from the viewpoint of the world, and the world listens to them. *6*I am grateful that since I am from you O' God, that I and your other children can recognize and understand each other for the reason that we know you, but whoever is not from you disregards us. This is how I can recognize the Spirit of Truth and the spirit of falsehood.

*7*Dear Father, encourage me to love others, for love comes from you. Let me not forget that everyone who loves has been born of you and knows you. *8*If I do not have love, I do not know you, because you are love. *9*Thank you Lord for showing your love to me by sending your one and only Son Jesus into the world so that I might live through him. *10*Help me grasp that love is not that I loved you, but that you loved me and sent Jesus as an atoning sacrifice for my sins. *11*I pray that since you so loved me, I would also love others. *12*I recognize that no one has ever seen you Lord; but help me to realize that if I love others, you live in me and your love is made complete in me.

*13 & 14*Bless you Lord for showing me that I live in you and you in me by the Holy Spirit and by the witness that you have sent Jesus to be the Savior of the world. *15 & 16*Heavenly Father illuminate for me, that if I acknowledge that Jesus is your Son, you will live in me and I will live in you; this is how I will know and rely on the love you have for me. *17*Help me realize that this is the way that love is made complete in me so that I will have confidence on the Day of Judgment, because in this world I am like you.

*18*May I always bear in mind that there is no fear in love. Perfect love drives out fear, because fear has to do with punishment. If I am the one who fears then I am not made perfect in love. *19*I worship you Mighty God because you first loved me. *20 & 21*Master help me understand that if I say "I love God" and yet hate my brother, I am a liar. For if I do not love my brother, whom I have seen, I cannot love you, whom I have not seen and let me also keep in mind that you have given me this command: Whoever loves God must also love his brother!

5/Father I believe that Jesus is the Christ, born of you. I love you Father and your son Jesus, as well as all your other children. *2*This is how I can know that I love the children of God: by loving you and carrying out your commands. *3*May I always keep in mind that my love for you is to obey your commands and your commands are not burdensome. *4*I pray that you keep me ever conscious that everyone born of God overcomes the world and that the victory that overcomes the world is my faith. *5*Encourage me to answer the question "Who is it that overcomes the world?" with the truth that everyone who believes that Jesus is the Son of God overcomes the world.

*6*I thank you Jesus because you are the one who came by water and blood. You did not come by water only, but by water and blood and it is the Holy Spirit who testifies of this, because the Spirit is the truth. *7 & 8*Allow me to grasp that there are three that testify: the Holy Spirit, the water and the blood; and the three are in agreement. *9*Master I accept man's testimony, but your testimony is greater because it is your testimony which you have given about Jesus. *10*Keep me mindful I pray, that if anyone believes in the Son of God they have this testimony in their heart. Likewise anyone who does not believe; you Mighty God have made them out to be a liar, because they have not believed the testimony you have given about your son Jesus. *11*Cause me to often consider that this is the testimony: That you O' God have given me eternal life and this life is in your son Jesus. *12*I worship you my King because he who has the Son has life; he who does not have the Son of God does not have life.

[13]I am forever indebted to you Jesus for it is written: that if I believe in the name of the Son of God, I may know that I have eternal life. [14 &] [15]Thank you Father God for the confidence I have in approaching you. Thank you for knowing that if I ask anything according to your will, you hear me and since I know that you hear me; whatever I ask, I know that I will have what I have asked of you.

[16]Encourage me Master that if I see a brother commit a sin that does not lead to death, I should pray and you will give him life. Since there is a sin that leads to death; illuminate for me that I need not pray about that. [17]Lord keep me conscious that all wrongdoing is sin, but that there are sins that do not lead to death. [18]Praise you my King, since I am born of you I will not continue to sin because Jesus will keep me safe and the evil one cannot harm me

[19]I know that I am one of your children and that the whole world is under the control of the evil one. [20]I also know that you Jesus have come to give me understanding, so that I may know Him who is true. Bless you Mighty God because in your Son Jesus Christ I am in the One who is true and who is the eternal life. [21]Dear Father, always keep me from idols.

REFLECTIONS

The Book of 2nd John

1 *1-2*Bless you Jesus, because not only have you shown me the truth, but because the truth lives in me and will be with me forever. *3*Thank you God my Father for the grace, mercy and peace that is through your Son Jesus Christ, who is with me in truth and love. *4*I pray Father that you give me great joy from walking in the truth, just as you have commanded. *5*I realize that this is not a new command, but the one I have had from the beginning which is; to love others. *6*Help me to understand that love is walking in obedience to your commands and your command is; that I walk in love.

*7*I pray that you keep me ever aware that many deceivers, who do not acknowledge Jesus Christ as coming in the flesh, have gone out into the world and any such person is the deceiver and the antichrist. *8*Guide me Holy Spirit, to keep a watch out so that I do not lose what I have worked for and for which I will be fully rewarded. *9*I call upon you Jesus, to help me remember that I must never run ahead and I must continue in your teaching, because if I do not continue in your teaching I have neither you, nor my Father. *10-11* Keep me vigilant that if anyone comes to me and does not bring your teaching; I should not take them into my house or even welcome them, because anyone who welcomes them shares in their wicked work.

REFLECTIONS

_____

_____

_____

_____

_____

_____

_____

The Book of 3rd John

1 *²*Lord, I pray for the brethren and myself that we may enjoy good health and that all may go well with us, even as our souls are getting along well. *³*I also pray that we would continue to walk in faithfulness to the truth. *⁴*Help me to realize that there is no greater joy than walking in the truth. *⁵*Keep me faithful in what I do for missionaries, even though they may seem like strangers to me. *⁶⁻⁷*Let me not forget that I would do well to send them on their way in a manner worthy of you, since it was for Your Namesake that they go out, receiving no help from the pagans. *⁸*Remind me often to show hospitality to such workers, so that I may participate with them in the work of spreading the truth. *¹¹*I ask that you would show me daily how to imitate what is good and not what is evil. Keep it clear in my mind that anyone who does what is good is from you and anyone who does what is evil has not seen you.

REFLECTIONS

_____

_____

_____

_____

_____

_____

_____

_____

_____

_____

_____

_____

The Book of Jude

1 *¹ & ²*As your servant Lord Jesus and as a brother of those who have been called, who are loved by God the Father, may mercy, peace and love always be ours in abundance. *³*Urge me to always be very eager to share the salvation I have received and to contend for the faith that was once and for all entrusted to the saints. *⁴*I am persuaded that certain men, whose condemnation was written about long ago, have secretly slipped in among the church. These godless men change your grace into a license for immorality and deny that you, Jesus, are our only Sovereign and Lord.

*⁵*Even though I already know this, I want you to remind me often that you delivered your people out of Egypt, but later destroyed those who did not believe. *⁶*Let me never forget that the angels who did not keep their positions of authority, but abandoned their own home are being kept in darkness, bound with everlasting chains for judgment on the great Day. *⁷*I pray that you keep me conscious that in a similar way, Sodom and Gomorrah gave themselves up to sexual immorality and perversion and now they serve as an example of those who suffer the punishment of eternal fire.

*⁸*Let me not be surprised Jesus, that in the very same way there will be apostates who will pollute their own bodies, reject authority and slander celestial beings. *⁹*May I regularly think about the fact that even the archangel Michael, when he was disputing with the devil about the body of Moses, did not dare to bring a slanderous accusation against him, but said, "The Lord rebuke you!" *¹⁰*Yet there are those who speak abusively against whatever they do not understand; and what things they do understand by instinct, like unreasoning animals; these are the very things that destroy them.

*¹¹*Illuminate for me my Master the woe that is due them because they have taken the way of Cain; they have rushed for profit into Balaam's error; they have been destroyed as in Korah's rebellion. *¹²*Help me to grasp that men like these are blemishes at the Christians' love feasts:

eating without the slightest qualm, they are shepherds who feed only themselves. Let me see that they are clouds without rain, blown along by the wind; autumn trees, without fruit and uprooted that are twice dead. [13]They are wild waves of the sea, foaming up their shame; wandering stars, for whom blackest darkness has been reserved forever.

[14 & 15]Help me also realize that this truth is further substantiated by Enoch (who was the seventh from Adam), when he prophesied about these men by saying: "See, the Lord is coming with thousands upon thousands of his holy ones to judge everyone, and to convict all the ungodly of all the ungodly acts they have done in the ungodly way, and of all the harsh words ungodly sinners have spoken against him." [16]May I be quick to recognize that these type of men are grumblers and faultfinders; they follow their own evil desires; they boast about themselves and flatter others for their own advantage.

[17 & 18] Compel me Lord Jesus to remember that you foretold this when you said, "In the last times there will be scoffers who will follow their own ungodly desires." [19]These type of men will try to divide us Christians; they follow mere natural instincts and do not have the Spirit. [20]Keep me mindful that I should build myself up in my most holy faith and pray in the Holy Spirit. [21]May I always keep myself in your love as I wait for your mercy to bring me to eternal life. [22 & 23]Teach me to be merciful to those who doubt, to snatch others from the fire and save them and to others show mercy, mixed with fear, but hating even the clothing stained by corrupted flesh. [24] Finally, to you my King, who is able to keep me from falling and to present me before your glorious presence without fault and with great joy. [25]To you my only God and Savior be glory, majesty, power and authority, through Jesus Christ my Lord, before all ages, now and forevermore!

REFLECTIONS

REFLECTIONS

REFLECTIONS

REFLECTIONS

Printed in the United States
By Bookmasters